CAREER REINVENTION

A Path to Fulfillment, Wealth, and Giving Back

Discovering New Opportunities, Building Passive
Income, and Making a Difference with
Meaningful Impact

(Living Beyond 9-5)

Dennis J. Dwyre

Contents

Introduction

Greetings, my friend.

The information you are about to consume discloses a path to *Career Reinvention*.

Many of the topics we cover contain options you can quickly and easily implement.

Whether you're currently unemployed, seeking a higher-paying position in your field, considering a career change, or exploring new income streams, this book provides the ideas and inspiration to ignite your imagination.

Please suspend any disbelief in your abilities as you explore the possibilities set out before you. I encourage *you* to permit yourself to be the person you want to be. As the captain of your ship, you are entirely able to chart your own course. What you set your mind to do, you can surely accomplish.

If you are a financial provider for your household, you are responsible for supporting yourself and those who depend on you. Being a financial provider is a huge responsibility and can be challenging in this fast-paced, ever-changing world. It is common practice these days to reinvent yourself as new technologies and other economic factors come into play. Therefore, I have included a proven goal achievement strategy to assist you with this challenge.

I call it the DAPVEA method of goal completion. It results from a thirty-plus-year focus on how we naturally achieve our goals. This goal-achievement method is an innate process as ancient as human life itself and *is* the original manifesting technique. When all six steps of the strategy are used in conjunction, they dramatically increase your likelihood of achieving a desire and breaking free into a completely new way of life.

The DAPVEA method can be identified within the lives of the successful people used as examples in this book. These ultra-successful people have various ways of bringing home the bacon, and we will be taking a deep dive into some of the actions they took to reinvent their careers. These extraordinary people recognize that they have options regarding how they create income, wealth, and time freedom. You also have options.

Now is the time to open your mind to a new way of thinking regarding your career. You may choose to work in a company—large or small—not as an owner but as an employee. You may possess the skills to earn a lot of money on this path, and many people are excited to be doing so.

For your convenience, helpful links to large corporate trade organizations are provided in Chapter 4. These resources will unlock multiple doors of opportunity in your hunt for more suitable employment, whether you apply these specific leads or not.

You may choose to be self-employed. A multitude of career possibilities can be found on this path, some of which can be tapped into with the help of our modern-day internet. You'll be the CEO of a business you created and assume responsibility for its success. The risks of this path are more significant than with the paycheck job, but the rewards can also be greater.

No matter how you earn your daily bread, your endgame should be to develop a stream of passive income, which is money that comes to you each month with minimal effort on your part. This is known as "putting your money to work for you." Such income could be from royalties, stocks, rents, or any other asset others will pay to buy or use. Putting your money to work for you is the rich man's way of building wealth. It will eventually allow you to jump off the employee and business income treadmill. Once you develop enough passive income to where your finances have reached what is called critical mass, you'll never have to work another day in your life—unless you want to.

With the excess funds gained from your business interests and passive income, you can climb the ladder to become a value investor or venture capitalist. This level of investing is highly speculative and has much in common with gambling, so you'll want to practice extreme due diligence before tossing any of your hard-earned money in that direction, especially if your goal is capital preservation.

Charitable giving and philanthropy are the obvious endgame of career reinvention. The act of giving can be used as a powerful motivational tool to spurn you onward to producing even greater wealth from the various ventures you engage in. One of life's most purpose-filled missions is helping others live healthier, happier lives. By donating your time, treasure, or both, you can make your mark on your community and leave the world a better place than you found it.

The path ahead is the one you choose. This book will help you make the choices that are right for you.

Ready? Let's get to work!

Chapter 1

Take Inventory of Your Career

Do you remember when you were a kid and your teacher asked what you wanted to be when you grew up?

Sitting there at your mini desk, your response was limited only by your imagination. Your answer could be anything! Astronaut, doctor, inventor, or movie star—while your choice may have been ambitious, it was what captured your heart at that time.

As you got older, reality reared its ugly head. You learned that life was competitive, and you had to make hard decisions about how you wanted to earn your living. As you began to make these decisions, you began to realize these early career choices may shape the rest of your life.

Some people choose a career path early and never deviate from it. A good example of an early chooser is Mary Barra, the president and CEO of General Motors. She landed her first job at GM when she was just 18 years old as a fender and hood inspector. She discovered she loved the automobile industry, specifically GM. Since that day, she's worked nowhere else.

With never a thought of making a career change, this go-getter rose through the ranks—a true "GM lifer"—until she reached the top.

She happens to be a trailblazer—she's the first female CEO of a Big Three automaker in history. Before Mary Barra, it was unthinkable that a woman would helm a car company. No way! But at some point in her career at GM, Mary Barra said to herself, "You know what? I could be the CEO of this company! It could really happen!" From that moment on, she conducted herself as a future leader. She wasn't the top leader but carried herself the same way any male rising executive would. And when the time came, the board of GM looked at Mary Barra and said, "She's our next leader."

Mary Barra is an exception. In fact, like many young people, when you were 18, you may have had no clue about what you wanted to do with your life. So you randomly chose a major in college, or you applied for a job just because it was available. You worked in a particular industry for a while, realized it was not what you wanted, and switched to another career path. There's nothing wrong with this! The more experience you have in different jobs and industries, the wider your horizon.

John Glenn was an ace Marine Corps combat aviator who joined the space program and, in 1962, became the first American astronaut to orbit Earth. But 12 years later, at 53 years old, he entered politics and became a U.S. senator in Ohio, a role he held for 24 years.

Martha Stewart was a fashion model who, in 1967, at the age of 26, launched a career as a stockbroker, which was her father-in-law's profession. She worked on Wall Street until 1976, when she started a catering business at age 35 in the basement of her Westport, Connecticut home. The business took off, and in 1982, she released her first book, *Entertaining*. More books followed, and then a magazine and television program. On the cover of their May 1995 issue, *New York Magazine* declared Stewart "the definitive American woman of our time."

There are many more such people who, having found success in one industry or profession, made a big change—and found even more success.

Changing Jobs vs. Careers

It's common knowledge that most workers change jobs frequently. If you look at Mary Barra, even though she's worked at General Motors her entire adult life, you'll see she's changed jobs many times. After holding various engineering and administrative positions, including managing the Detroit/Hamtramck Assembly plant, she became vice president of Global Manufacturing Engineering. She then advanced to the position of vice president of Global Human Resources and then executive vice president of Global Product Development before being named chief executive officer.

Did she change jobs because she was unhappy or dissatisfied with her career? No. She changed jobs because she loved the auto industry, loved GM, and wanted more responsibility. She found her calling and had no thought of making a career change.

This is why it's important to understand the distinction between changing jobs and changing your career.

Changing your career means entering a new line of work requiring different skills and training. If you're a lawyer and at the age of 40 you decide to become a full-time forest ranger, that's a career change. If you're an insurance agency manager and decide to start a company designing electric cars, that's a career change.

If you jump from one job to another in the same industry, that's not a career change. To go back to Mary Barra, imagine if she had taken the position of VP of Global Manufacturing Engineering at GM. Then, after a few years in that role, it became clear to her that she would not be promoted higher up the executive ladder. The doors were closed. But she liked her job and wanted more responsibility. Then she heard of an opening in the C-suite at Ford Motor Company. The job represented a promotion, so she applied, was hired, and worked at Ford.

Did she experience a midlife crisis about her career path? Had she grown tired of working in the auto industry and wanted a change of pace?

The answer is "no" on both counts. In fact, she loved her career and, to keep growing in it, had to jump ship from one employer to another. She would be changing jobs, not her career.

Tracking how often people change jobs is tricky, but there's some reliable data. According to

Zippia.com, the average American worker has 12 different jobs during their lifetime, and 65 percent of American workers are actively searching for a new full-time job right now.

According to the U.S. Bureau of Labor Statistics, in January 2022, the median number of years that wage and salary workers had been with their current employer was 4.1 years, unchanged from the median in January 2020. It's important to note that job tenure varies with the industry. For example, in January 2022, wage and salary workers in the public sector had a median term of 6.8 years, much higher than the median of 3.7 years for private-sector employees. Federal government employees had a higher median tenure (7.5 years) than state (6.3 years) or local government (6.9 years) employees.

Among the major private industries, workers in manufacturing had the highest tenure, at 5.2 years. By contrast, workers in leisure and hospitality had the lowest median tenure, at 2.0 years. Many of these variations are due to age: workers in leisure and hospitality tend to be younger and more likely to switch jobs.

As people get older, they change jobs less frequently. Between 18 and 24, people change jobs an average of 5.7 times. The average number of job changes between 25 and

34 years old is 2.4. From 35 to 44, the average decreases to 2.9 jobs, and then to 1.9 jobs from 45 to 52.

Remember, these statistics are counting people who change jobs. They do not reveal how many have changed careers, which means a much more significant life alteration.

At what age do people change careers? According to CNBC.com, the average age a person changes careers is 39 years old. This is because workers in mid-career may feel stagnated, spurring them to make a career switch for new opportunities.

Why People Change Careers

A survey by Indeed.com sought to find out *why* people changed careers.

The top five reasons why workers changed careers were:

1. Unhappy in previous job or sector: 81 percent

2. Wanted greater flexibility: 79 percent

3. Wanted to earn more money: 79 percent

4. Did not feel challenged or satisfied: 78 percent

5. Wanted more opportunities for advancement: 77 percent.

You can see that the total percentages add up to much more than 100 percent, which means the respondents chose multiple reasons for wanting a change.

Note the word "unhappy" in the first reason. It's important to consider what this might mean. It might mean the usual job-related reasons, such as bad workplace culture or unreasonable bosses. But it may also mean the person was simply bored or unfulfilled by the work and wanted a change. People often take a job because nothing else is available, they're qualified, and they need the money. After a few years, they ask themselves, "Is this what I want to do for the rest of my life?" The answer is often "No."

Take Stock of Your Life

Here's a question worth pondering: If you could pursue any vocation without regard to what it paid, what would it be?

As you think about this, consider how you feel about your current job and career path. There are some definite signs indicating it's time for a change. They may include:

- **You dread going to work.** Instead of waking up in the morning with a happy heart and looking forward to the challenges and opportunities of your vocation, you think, "Ugh—another day in the salt mines."

- **You're complacent and apathetic.** The new catchphrase is "quiet quitting." According to Gallup and other pollsters, quiet quitters make up at least 50 percent of the U.S. workforce. It means that you're doing exactly what's required to earn your paycheck, and not a scintilla more.

- **You don't feel like you're making a difference.** You say to yourself, "I'm just a pencil pusher. No one cares what I do. I come to work, do my job, and when I leave, the world looks just the same."

- **Your job is a drag on your personal life.** When you come home after a day of work, you don't walk into the house with a sense of pride or accomplishment. You struggle to be in a good mood because you're not happy—and your family can feel it.

- **The greenbacks have lost their luster.** While money is important, it can't make up for a boring job. "Golden handcuffs are the financial security, comfort and safety of high-paying, cushy jobs that are unfulfilling in some way or all ways, or downright miserable-making," says Sara DiVello, author of *Where in the OM Am I? One Woman's Journey from the Corporate World to the Yoga Mat.* "But they keep us bound to our desks and offices because we become dependent on them or scared to leave or addicted to the various aspects of a fast-paced, high-stress career."[1]

Does that describe how you feel? Afraid to lose the golden handcuffs because of financial insecurity? Maybe it's time to

---

[1] Forbes. https://www.forbes.com/sites/laurashin/2014/02/03/cant-leave-a-miserable-job-because-of-the-money-take-these-7-steps/?sh=46e94cb73069

divest yourself of costly assets that force you to keep "feeding the meter."

- **You daydream about a new career.** It's fine to imagine yourself in a better job, but if you're consumed by detailed fantasies about handing your boss your two weeks' notice and walking out the door, these daydreams could signal that you need a new job—or a career change. It may be time to take action and turn those daydreams into reality.

- **You constantly work long hours with overtime—and don't like it.** There's an old saying: "If you hate working overtime at your current job, then quit, open your own business, and work even longer hours." Do you know what? Countless entrepreneurs are doing exactly that, and they could not be happier. It's very difficult to work long hours at a job you hate. Working long hours gives you less time to exercise, prepare healthy meals, relax, and just enjoy life. Studies have shown that people who work overtime may have increased alcohol consumption and body mass index, which may exacerbate other health problems.

Putting in excessive hours can also hurt your mental health. Spending more time on the 9-5 treadmill and worrying about your career increases stress levels. It heightens the risk of anxiety, depression, and mental health issues. It puts stress on personal relationships, which increases your risk of depression and increases the risk of familial conflict. When one or both partners in a marriage consistently work overtime, the chances of divorce increase.

In Japan, long notorious for its culture of overwork, there's a name for it. *Karoshi* literally means "death by overwork," and it's a real phenomenon. The most common medical causes of karoshi deaths are heart attacks and strokes due to stress and malnourishment or fasting. Mental stress from the workplace can also cause *karoshi* through workers taking their own lives. People who die by suicide due to overwork are called *karōjisatsu*. The phenomenon of death by overwork is also widespread in other parts of Asia. In 2016, the World Health Organization reported 745,194 deaths worldwide attributable to long working hours.

If you're working to develop a career you love and working something close to normal hours, it'll seem like you're getting paid to have fun. The time will fly past, and you'll end each day tired but happy.

You Deserve a Bigger Paycheck

Sometimes, you can be paid generously and still hate your job. But your situation may be different: perhaps you're being underpaid, affecting how you feel about your job and even your job performance.

According to a March 2022 survey conducted by Qualtrics on behalf of Credit Karma, of more than 2,000 American workers polled, two-thirds said their pay was inadequate to cover the rising cost of inflation. Aside from inflation, nearly 30 percent felt they were not paid fairly at work. Of the respondents, 33 percent of women reported feeling underpaid, compared to 25 percent of men.[2]

Even people earning over $100,000 a year may have trouble making ends meet. A survey by LendingClub found that the number of consumers living paycheck to paycheck has increased steadily and, in January 2022, hit 64 percent. Perhaps surprisingly, 48 percent of consumers earning more than $100,000 per year reported living without significant savings, and 67 percent of middle-income consumers earned between $50,000 and $100,000 a year.

These paycheck-to-paycheck consumers fall into two categories: those who can pay their bills (42 percent) and those who struggle to pay their bills (22 percent). In addition, many households say they could not pay an emergency expense of just four hundred dollars.[3]

The Cost of Not Taking Action

Many people, perhaps yourself included, are unhappy with their current careers but focus on the perceived cost of making a change—the temporary loss of income, having to start over at a lower rung on the ladder, or needing more

---

[2] https://www.creditkarma.com/about/commentary/inflation-brings-to-the-fore-pay-inequities-this-equal-pay-day
[3] https://ir.lendingclub.com/news/news-details/2022/48-Percent-of-Americans-with-Annual-Incomes-over-100000-Live-Paycheck-to-Paycheck-9-percentage-points-higher-than-first-reported-in-June-2021/default.aspx

education. The obsession with these costs can convince someone that making a change isn't worth the price.

But you owe it to yourself to look at the problem from a different perspective: the cost of maintaining the status quo. How miserable are you willing to be? If you do nothing, your mental and physical health may suffer. A study from Ohio State University found that employees who expressed lower levels of fulfillment in their careers were more likely to also report issues like depression or sleep difficulty. "The higher levels of mental health problems for those with low job satisfaction may be a precursor to future physical problems," said Hui Zheng, a sociology professor at OSU and author of the study. "Increased anxiety and depression could lead to cardiovascular or other health problems that won't show up until they are older."[4]

A study of over 24,000 workers in Japan found that job dissatisfaction was predictive of poor health among middle-aged workers. Policymakers and managers were encouraged to monitor the job dissatisfaction of their employees and improve their work environments to enhance their occupational health.[5]

---

[4] OSU. https://news.osu.edu/lousy-jobs-hurt-your-health-by-the-time-youre-in-your-40s/

[5] Oshio T. Job dissatisfaction as a predictor of poor health among middle-aged workers: a 14-wave mixed model analysis in Japan. *Scand J Work Environ Health*. 2021 Nov 1;47(8):591-599. doi: 10.5271/sjweh.3985. Epub 2021 Sep 14. PMID: 34518892; PMCID: PMC9058618.

Researchers from the Financial Consumer Agency of Canada found that, for many families, money worries are the greatest source of stress—even more than work, personal health, and relationships. Their research showed that 48 percent of those surveyed said they'd lost sleep because of financial worries, and 44 percent said it would be difficult to meet their financial obligations if their pay were late. If you are dealing with financial stress, the researchers found that you're four times as likely to suffer from sleep problems, headaches, and other illnesses, twice as likely to report poor overall health, and more likely to experience strain in your personal relationships. Financial stress can also lead to more serious health problems, such as high blood pressure, heart disease, and mental health conditions, such as anxiety and depression.[6]

Analyze Your Mindset

Taking inventory of your employment position reveals the level of satisfaction you have with your present occupation. Here are some questions and practical steps to take when analyzing your mindset after the inventory process.

Put aside any guilt. This may seem like an odd thing to say, but your first priority is to make yourself #1. You deserve better! Don't feel guilty about leaving a job that no longer meets your needs. If the tables were turned and your

---

[6] https://www.canada.ca/en/financial-consumer-agency/services/financial-wellness-work/stress-impacts.html

employer no longer needed you, they would show you the door in the blink of an eye!

Identify barriers. Identify and describe the psychological obstacles preventing you from reinventing your career. Examples could be fear of losing a secure income, pension, or other benefits, losing power or prestige, the desire to live up to an image of loyalty and success, or not knowing how to begin a new career search.

Know you have choices. How much of a change do you want to make? You may want to change departments in the same organization, move to a new occupational field, become a self-employed entrepreneur, take a sabbatical, or even return to school for continuing education. Check the FAFSA program at your chosen college: you may qualify for free schooling.

Plan your budget. If you want to return to school or start your own business and are concerned about having a reduced income, you can begin by temporarily restructuring your existing loans. Make a list of all your debts, from smallest to largest, and begin paying off these debts one by one. Getting free of high-interest consumer debt will change your whole financial outlook. With the resulting increased cashflow, build up a two- to three-month expenses savings cushion, and most importantly—choose a job with business hours that won't conflict with your schooling activities.

Accept that change involves tradeoffs. Making a job or career change may involve some temporary personal or financial sacrifices. But in the long term, achieving your goal will far outweigh any losses. You'll enjoy greater career satisfaction, financial independence, and control over your personal and work lives.

Don't stay in a low-wage job because of security. In today's volatile job market, where employer loyalty to employees is nearly a thing of the past, job security is wishful thinking. You can probably think of a number of reasons to stay in an unfulfilling career, but deciding to stay can be as traumatic as turning in your notice and moving along.

Listen to what your body is telling you. If your current line of work requires a great deal of physical activity, be aware that your physical capabilities will decrease as you age, which could disrupt many of your best-made plans in retirement.

Don't fear failure. This is the most important thing of all. Setbacks are learning experiences. Successful changers do fail, and when they do, they say, "I've done my best—I'm only human—and I'm going to get up and try again."

Confirm your feelings. If an inventory and analysis of your mindset surrounding your work life has made you uncomfortable, this is a sign you are yearning for an upgrade. If you have experienced mild discontent during this inventory, a few added income streams may be the change you are looking for. In either case, please take note of your feelings. Whether you act on them or not, they hold enormous meaning for your future.

The following chapter has been placed early in the book as a bridge to help take you from where you are now to where you want to be. This easily implemented goal achievement method has a very successful track record—you use portions of it on a daily basis without even realizing it.

Chapter 2

Embrace the DAPVEA Method

The solution to transforming your career is tapping into the boundless potential that already resides within you.

What is this boundless potential, you ask? It's called the DAPVEA method. By the way, the DAPVEA acronym represents the first letter of each step of our innate six-step goal achievement process.

The world is run by the DAPVEA method. This is a bold claim to make, but once you've completed this chapter, you'll understand why I say it is so.

As you look back on any of your achieved goals, you will discover that the DAPVEA method was a part of the process.

Take a moment to reflect on a goal you have accomplished and are happy with.

Now, compare that goal process to the following six steps.

1. When you originally set out to accomplish said goal, did you first have a *desire* for it?

2. Did you begin thinking *auto-suggestions* such as, "I'd like to figure out a way to get one of those"?

3. Had you silently or audibly recited *positive affirmations* such as, "I am finding a way to acquire my desire"?

4. Had you *visualized* some of the processes and results of achieving your desire?

5. Were *emotions and/or feelings* involved in bringing your desire to fruition?

6. Did you take a series of mental and physical *actions* to achieve your desire?

Don't be misled into believing the DAPVEA method is delusional thinking due to the fact that some of our desires bypass portions of the six-step process. A habit may only require a desire and a visualization for the habit to be acted upon. In contrast, the original desire that produced the habit will have been accomplished through the six-step goal completion method.

When you revisit the early beginnings of any particular behavior, good or bad, you will understand that the DAPVEA method is soft-wired into our very being. As you compare the processes of any achieved goal to the steps contained within the DAPVEA method, you will realize that a number of the boxes are checked, most likely all six.

To help increase your awareness of the DAPVEA method, let's explore the applications of the innate six steps we take to manifest a desire.

Desire

A lot of the information available on desire quickly morphs into a deep contemplation about where our desires originate or why we desire. We aren't going down those two rabbit holes; instead, we will focus on recognizing desire as the genesis point for transforming our careers. We will also explore a few advanced techniques of tapping into this powerful energy source called desire, via the DAPVEA method.

There is a fine line between a want and a desire. A want is a weak feeling of wishing for something. A desire is an intense feeling that gets acted upon in some way. A strong desire fosters enthusiasm, joy, and a sense of purpose, while a want perpetuates the opposite.

If you do not have a clearly defined career desire at this time, read through this entire book to gather ideas and inspiration. Then, return to this chapter and begin afresh with your chosen career desire.

If you already have a career goal or higher line of income in mind, your next move is clarification. With clarity, you can remove the fog around your desire, and chart a course that will allow you to break the chains of your current paradigm.

Before launching into the desire clarification process, free your mind of the burdens and negativity of current life. Dwell only on positive thoughts and circumstances. Now, focus on an end result of your desire and act as if you already possess your dream job. Continue to dwell on the desire until ideas appear about how to achieve it.

Make time for this exercise, knowing that these small beginnings are crucial to reinventing your career.

As far as tomorrow and the upcoming days are concerned, I challenge you to play pretend each day until you develop a new self-concept that includes the changes you are seeking.

If you persist in acting as if you are already this new person, your desire, or something similar, will become an eventual certainty.

Be prepared for some not-so-comfortable situations to arise as you move toward this new version of yourself. Combat these growth challenges by re-focusing your attention back on your original desire. Bear with these situations because they are a necessary part of your desire becoming fulfilled.

One last thing before we move on to the second step of the DAPVEA method: if you are serious about creating a new future for yourself, write down your desire along with the ideas that come from dwelling on it. These original ideas are compelling inspirations when referred to regularly. They will also become the basis for a persuasive auto-suggestion.

Auto-Suggestion

Our auto-suggestions are often a spontaneous reaction to external stimuli. An example of a reaction to external stimuli is when we see a nice car and say to ourselves, "I'd like to have one of those." The auto-suggestions we are dealing with in this book are not reactions to external stimuli but declarations we manufacture due to our desire to reinvent our careers.

The auto-suggestion "I'd kind of like to find a better job" reveals a shallow commitment to a desire. Reciting "I'm finding a better job" shows an increased level of commitment. Reciting "I'm finding a better job now" reveals a tremendous amount of commitment to your desire. The latter type of high-vibrational inputs are what we are after when it comes to creating effective auto-suggestions.

Here are some helpful hints on the use of auto-suggestions.

1. **Use habitual, repetitive tasks as an opportunity to reprogram yourself.** Recite positive auto-suggestions while showering, working, exercising, or commuting.

2. **Recite positive auto-suggestions until it hurts.** Verbally recite your chosen auto-suggestion until a wash of feelings comes over you. Some of these feelings will consist of time, destiny, and mortality. When these feelings appear, continue to recite your auto-suggestion for a few more minutes to help integrate it into your inner being. This process is amazing. You can actually feel yourself changing into the topic of your auto-suggestion.

3. **Stop self-sabotage by replacing negativity with positive auto-suggestions.** Be mindful of your self-talk. If you indulge in negative self-talk and allow thoughts of fear, doubt, or guilt, delete those thoughts by reciting the phrase, "That's not part of my belief system."

Another technique for removing negative thoughts was discovered by artists as a treatment for procrastination. Many of these artists believe that negative thoughts come from what has been termed our *Inner Critic*. The Inner Critic is a mischievous rascal who likes to cause confusion and failure. To strip this villain of his power, tell the Inner Critic to get lost and don't come back.

When the previous techniques fail to rid you of negative thoughts, your higher power must be called on to subdue the Inner Critic. The following information may be considered controversial to some people, but after a couple of years of struggling with the nature of negative thoughts, I began to understand that the Inner Critic boils down to a negative force. And where do negative forces originate? The dark side, of course. So, with this in mind, say, "Satan, I command you to flee this temple of God in the name of the Father, Son, and Holy Spirit." I consider this technique the most effective way to remove persistent negative thoughts.

If you are experiencing negative thoughts and do not have the time and energy to fight this battle, get help. Many people suffer from mental conditions that have been caused through no fault of their own.

Research studies have proven that the number and severity of adverse childhood experiences, or ACEs, will influence the adult's emotional health. ACEs were first identified in the 1990s by the Centers for Disease Control and Prevention (CDC) and Kaiser Permanente, which together conducted the first ACEs study. The researchers asked more than 17,000 adults about their childhood experiences, including emotional, physical, and sexual abuse, neglect, and household challenges of parental separation, substance abuse, incarceration, violence, and mental illness. Researchers identified a link between the number and severity of ACEs and a higher likelihood of adverse health and behavioral outcomes later in life, such as heart disease, diabetes, and premature death.

If you determine that ACEs are inhibiting you from creating a prosperous life for yourself, consider professional counseling. Counseling can help you move from living in a negative past to living a life full of optimism and excitement. Optimism and excitement are valuable traits to lean on as you reinvent your career.

Positive Affirmation

The next natural step we take toward a goal or desire is to recite positive affirmations based on an auto-suggestion.

Notice when you say, "I want to reinvent my career," the obvious furtherance of that statement is, "I am reinventing my career somehow," or "I am reinventing my career now, no matter what." These positive affirmations, or PAs, are statements that align with a future quality you seek to possess.

Only a small fraction of the information on creating PAs suggests anything about impressing your subconscious so thoroughly that you will take autonomous measures toward your desire.

The subconscious mind operates much like a hard drive on a computer. The programming inside a hard drive stores and manages crucial information that dictates the computer's overall performance. Likewise, the positive affirmations that are impressed into your subconscious determine your overall performance.

An appropriately crafted PA will help you gain confidence, motivation, and self-esteem; if it doesn't, revisit the wording until you find a group of words that does. Energizing words such as *excited*, *enthusiastic*, *enthralled*, *elated*, and *ecstatic* will increase the potency of your affirmation.

To begin crafting an effective PA, start your PA with a humbling phrase and bring in the present tense. Next, state your desire with the end result in mind. If you believe in a higher power, following up your affirmation with the phrase "I praise God and have faith that it is so" is highly energetic. So, adhering to these universally accepted standards, a powerful positive affirmation will sound something like the following statement: "I'm so thankful, grateful, and excited now that I have found a more lucrative career; I praise God and have faith that it is so."

Develop a grouping of words that will roll off the tongue smoothly, and include a rhyme in the affirmation if you can. If it rolls off the tongue easily, the subconscious mind will more readily accept what is being stated.

Here are some helpful hints on the use of PAs:

- To increase the impact of your affirmation, say it out loud numerous times each day as if you are speaking what you desire into existence.

- Place notes and posters of your affirmation around your home or in your vehicle.

- Write out your PA in a journal until your hand hurts.

- Use the card technique: Write out your PA on a note card as a reminder and carry it with you wherever you go.

- Get excited about what your affirmations are doing to change your future.

The changing of our tomorrows is the end game of affirmations. As you consistently recite your PA, you will become your affirmation and will no longer need to recite it. The new qualities you possess will then be reflected back to you in ever-increasing quantities.

Visualization of Completed Goal

The fourth step of the DAPVEA method is literally out of this world. Think of this: We live in a three-dimensional world where everything has a length, width, and height. Now visualize your car, living space, or life mate. Can you measure your inner visualization in 3D? Nope, not going to happen. For the preceding observation to be accurate, your visualizations must exist in a different dimension—a dimension where anything is possible. Some visualizations only last microseconds or otherwise exist not as a picture in the mind but as a scene projected into thin air.

Visualizations within our imagination create our future. In the morning, we wake up and visualize drinking water, showering, or eating breakfast. We visualize getting to work on time. We visualize our next move at work and then the next. At quitting time, we visualize what we will do after work. We visualize our dinner and leisure time and then visualize going back to bed.

In certain instances, visualizations are a shortcut to the end result we are seeking, but only when we are dealing with familiar circumstances. However, concerning complex or unfamiliar matters, we typically ponder the situation until a visualization appears.

As with a positive affirmation, a visualization is also a projection of a future event. When we visualize something, our subconscious receives that impression as if it has already happened and begins moving toward realizing that impression. As our subconscious nudges toward the fulfillment of the impression, our desire, in turn, becomes more concrete.

Use the following process to create a visualization that will make an impact on your future:

- With your eyes closed, focus intensely on an end result of your desire.

- Create an imaginary scene or movie that aligns with the attainment of your desire.

- In this scene or movie, engage as many of your senses as possible.

For example, if you desire to increase your monthly income through investing, can you imagine an increased account balance reflected on your monthly statement? Can you feel the cash in your hand? Can you smell the money? Can you associate the increased cash flow with the sound of a cash register ringing? Can you imagine what could be done with this new money?

Visualizations can be difficult in some instances but do not worry about this minor detail. If you cannot readily produce a visualization of what you are after, affirm your objective instead. Your affirmations, when properly scripted, will eventually produce some type of image of your finished desire.

Your visualizations have immense power to create, but the feelings produced by visualizations hold even greater powers.

Emotion & Feeling States

The fifth step of the DAPVEA method is linking your desire, auto-suggestions, positive affirmations, and visualizations to feelings and emotions that motivate you.

This linking can easily be accomplished by internalizing joy or bliss when articulating through the preceding four steps. Note that the difference between an emotion and a feeling is its level of intensity and duration. For instance, joy can be an emotion when it is expressed in extreme instances, such as when your favorite sports team wins a championship. After the initial excitement of the win wanes, the emotion of joy becomes a feeling.

If you could step out of your body and observe your feelings and emotions, what would you see? Do you have a noble passion, or are you just passing through this world? Examining your feelings today can be a turning point in achieving your desires tomorrow because your feelings predetermine much of your life's happenings.

What motivates a musician to compose beautiful music, and why does an accountant love to work with numbers? Why do some people seek power and influence while others prefer to toil quietly, away from the public eye? It is because every human being is pulled one way or another by emotions and feeling states. The people who succeed at creating the life they desire do so through positive emotions and positive feeling states.

While rational calculation may provide a strategy for moving forward in life's pursuits, high vibrational feelings and emotions are the motivation for goal achievement. When we have mixed feelings about a desire, mixed results are what we get. A halfhearted desire for *Career Reinvention* will undoubtedly result in career and income stagnation.

Begin today to dwell on the feelings that arise from your desires. To better bring your feelings out of their hiding place, assume your desire is already achieved and ask yourself, "How do I feel now that my wish of finding a new career is fulfilled?" The answer to this question will become the driving force for your desire. Regularly focusing on these newly identified feelings will produce a compulsion to take action.

Be acutely aware that your conscious thoughts are responsible for the feelings embedded in your subconscious. Consumerism and immediate gratification are the downfall of many individuals. Is *your* day consumed with low vibrational inputs like social media or television? Or are you tapping into positive inputs that uplift your mood? If you are expecting real change to come about, you'll need to take a hard look at your choices, because these choices have long-lasting consequences.

Have you ever encountered someone who is faced with losing a home or even death but continues on their current path of destruction because they feel like it? As these people edge ever closer to losing everything, they tend to wake up a bit and realize their negative feelings and emotions are controlling them. By that time, it's too late.

Don't be that person; you have the power to control your conscious mind, your emotions, your feeling states, and the outputs from your subconscious—a change of impressions results in a change of expressions.

If your emotions and feeling states are not producing the results you are after, it is time to reevaluate your progress toward your objective. Think of this reevaluation as a necessary ingredient of your wish becoming fulfilled.

First, check your feelings about your desire and your feelings about the world as a whole. These feelings and emotions must all be positive. Flip any negativity around by replaying hurtful scenes in your life and change how you feel about them. Forgive those who have hurt you. You are only damaging yourself by clinging to negative feelings from the past.

Second, detach from any specific outcome of your desire by releasing the responsibility of its completion to your higher power or infinite intelligence. Consider yourself to be lacking nothing. Adopt an attitude that it is not your problem whether the desire comes to fruition or not, because you have a number of other options to fulfill it. This method may sound absolutely ridiculous, but it works.

Releasing your want does not mean stopping your visualizations, feeling states, and actions toward your desire. On the contrary, periodically take mental actions to produce imaginal feelings and visualizations that you do indeed possess multiple other options to acquire your desire. This feeling state shows you are detached from the outcome of your desire.

A lot of unpacking needs to be done as you implement this technique, but it comes down to *assuming* your wish is fulfilled without having the feeling of *wanting* your wish to be fulfilled. Can you see how detachment removes the conflict that is set up when you are wanting something while assuming you already possess it? Remove this conflict with the detachment technique.

The feelings and emotions we use to achieve our desires are like the fuel we run in our vehicles. As long as there is fuel, there is a flame. When the fuel runs out, the vehicle ceases to operate. The best way to keep fuel to your dreams of a better life is to dwell on the feelings associated with your desire as you retire for the night. This procedure is more fully explained in the upcoming "action" section.

Action

Take action today toward *Career Reinvention*.

The pursuit of a desire requires both physical and mental actions. Physical action is easy to understand; it consists of you moving, or something moving in the material world around you.

Mental action, also known as cognition, is understanding through thoughts, experiences, and the senses. Your cognitive capacity is tied to the intake and retention of information and its influence on your behavior and actions. I ask you now to examine your current level of cognition. Can you absorb a new way of thinking that will change the very nature of who you are?

Mental action is far superior to physical action. It's where the saying "Work smarter, not harder" comes from. More wealth has been produced by the human mind than any physical action ever could.

Working smarter, not harder, means asking yourself questions once again. These questions will result in multiple possibilities—if your mind is open to change. If your mind is closed to change, it's game over, simple as that.

One question you can ask yourself is: what can I do *today* to pursue my dream of a more lucrative career? Take all the time you need for answers to appear, then write your thoughts down in a journal.

Many of the most valuable thoughts ever conceived by mankind seem to have popped out of thin air. On the surface, some of these thoughts appear so ludicrous that they are dispensed with immediately. Don't be so quick to pass judgment on the impressions you receive. There are times when infinite intelligence sends a test to see how you will respond to the advice you are being given.

If you are unwilling to tune in and take the input seriously, infinite intelligence won't take your success seriously. Begin to listen carefully to your thoughts and be prepared to do some things that are way out of the ordinary.

As mentioned earlier, now that you have become familiar with the issues surrounding your desire to reinvent your career, you will naturally gravitate to the following shortcut when using the DAPVEA method, if your desire is strong enough.

This cognitive exercise requires little physical effort, and I encourage you to try it for an extended period of time until it becomes a habit. This technique impresses your desire onto your subconscious while you sleep.

You may find this exercise an outlandish measure to accomplish your objective. But, can you remember a time in your life when you were so obsessed with a desire that as you drifted off to sleep, you pictured the desire and imagined how you would feel when you possessed that new car, house, or spouse? Do you think your late-evening obsession had an impact on the accomplishment of your desire? You can bet on it.

Falling asleep with the feeling of your wish fulfilled is an advanced technique of the DAPVEA method and the single most powerful action you can take to achieve a challenging desire. This process is as natural as eating an apple, but is overlooked for its importance to goal achievement.

By now, you surely realize how important your mental actions are to your success. These actions include crystallizing your desire into a strong feeling of having or being and capturing that feeling and holding onto it while visualizing an end result of your desire. Frequently perform this same mental exercise to construct a quick link in your neural network to a finished result of your desire.

Recreate this process as you are retiring for the night and use it as a primer for taking even more action toward your desire. The following protocol is a structured route to the "fall asleep assuming your wish is fulfilled" technique.

Every night before drifting off to sleep, spend ten to fifteen minutes affirming, visualizing, and feeling your wish is fulfilled. Lie in a position you would not normally fall asleep in so as not to drift off too quickly. Ask yourself, "How do I feel now that my wish is fulfilled?" Capture that feeling, hold on to it, and dwell on it until you fall into unconsciousness.

Regular use of this technique changes your self concept and gives you the confidence to confront challenges as they arise, as well as being a catalyst for mental and physical actions in the days to come.

Behind the DAPVEA method lies the invisible quantum field. A variety of experiments have been conducted that prove the quantum field exists. The quantum field is part of infinite intelligence. Specific experiments show that prayer or good vibes directed toward a glass of water will cause positive changes to the molecular structure of the water molecules. The water molecules react to energy, frequency, and vibration. How obvious is it that when we apply these same energies toward career reinvention, changes in the unseen world begin to occur to make our desire a reality?

I reiterate: The DAPVEA method is the natural avenue we take to achieve all our goals and desires. It has a lot in common with the law of attraction, but it is a complete model of goal achievement that has served humanity well since prehistoric times.

Desire + Auto-suggestion + Positive affirmation + Visualization of completed goal + Emotion + Action = Real, measurable results.

Embrace the DAPVEA method as a shortcut to the career you desire. The results obtained are commensurate with the effort exerted. The beauty of this goal achievement method is that it can be accessed right from where you now sit. As you make the DAPVEA method part of your daily routine, goals will be accomplished that were previously only daydreams, allowing you much more control over your time, finances, and future.

As you read the next chapter and beyond, I encourage you to keep an open mind, jot down a few notes, and reflect upon the DAPVEA method when you are intrigued with a possibility for *Career Reinvention.*

Chapter 3

Employment vs. Self-Employment vs. Passive Income

There are three roads you can take toward career reinvention. The roads are not mutually exclusive. They can be put together like lanes of a freeway, and while you're driving along, you can switch from one lane to another and simultaneously reap the benefits of multiple sources of income. Having these different financial lanes in your life will help provide income security if your main income stream suddenly evaporates.

It is no secret that most people in the lower income brackets rely on only one source of income: their job. If you depend on only a single source of income, wake up to the reality of that income stream drying up eventually. It doesn't take much for something to go wrong, and poof, your livelihood may be severely affected.

Having multiple sources of income is a simple solution to the solitary income stream syndrome, but only those aware of the pitfalls of a single source of income will heed this calling. Even some of the wealthy class never understand how volatile it is to rely on only one source of income, much to their detriment when that income stream becomes a dumpster fire. Bankruptcies and lawsuits typically follow along with losing their homes and sometimes long-term relationships.

Let's look at options for mitigating potential losses from relying only on one source of income. Briefly, the three roads are:

Employment

Whether you are on by the hour, receive a salary, or are paid by commission, being employed means working for a paycheck signed by your employer. Your employer might be the Sole Proprietor Mom & Pop shop down the street, a small LLC of some sort, a branch manager, or the board of directors of a massive global corporation.

As an employee, you have little say-so concerning the company's direction and business dealings. Your primary responsibility is to do your job. Salaried employees can have more influence within the company than by-the-hour or commissioned employees, but ultimately, all three only work to fulfill the business strategy set forth by the owners or shareholders.

One downside to being an employee is that you can be laid off or fired at any time.

In November 2022, Elon Musk paid $44 billion to buy 9.6 percent of the stock of Twitter. You might think, "9.6 percent?

Who cares?" But his 9.6 percent made him the biggest shareholder and the *de facto* King of Twitter. He had enough clout to summarily fire several longtime Twitter executives. Those escorted out of the building included chief executive Parag Agrawal, chief financial officer Ned Segal, general counsel Sean Edgett, and the company's head of legal policy, trust, and safety, Vijaya Gadde.

With the termination issue set to aside, it's possible to make a significant income as an employee. Earlier in the book, we talked about Mary Barra, the CEO of General Motors. Her boss is the board of GM. They pay her a reported base salary of $2.1 million per year. Her total compensation package in 2021 totaled $29 million—not too shabby!

At Microsoft, CEO Satya Nadella received $49.9 million in fiscal year 2021. And at Apple, in 2020, CEO Tim Cook received a total pay package of a whopping $265 million. Be assured that these high paid employees earned their income. In many cases they have done more than what was expected of them.

Being an employee is similar to performing a tightrope walking act every single day at work. To succeed as a paycheck employee, at whatever level, you need to be flexible enough to find common ground with share holders, other employees, and customer accounts.

If you enjoy being a team player during working hours and leaving your work behind when the whistle blows, then being an employee might be a good fit for you.

Self-Employment

The idea of owning and operating one or more businesses is wired into many of us from the beginning. As small children, we dream of opening a lemonade stand, having a mowing service, or starting a restaurant. Then, in only a decade or so, the idea of being self-employed begins to fade for many. This is because we can unknowingly become programmed into buying the idea of needing to get a secure job. Parents, schools, employers, and the government can perpetuate this limiting belief. You don't have to fall for pier pressure. Keep an open mind and choose your own career path.

Being self-employed does not necessarily mean you have no partners or stakeholders. If you're an entrepreneur launching a business, you'll probably have partners like Sergey Brin and Larry Page when they launched Google in 1996. You'll probably have investors; when Steve Jobs, Steve Wozniak, and Ronald Wayne founded Apple in 1976, their first "angel" investor was Mike Markkula, who kicked in $91,000 as well as securing a $250,000 line of credit from Bank of America. He recruited his friend and former co-worker Michael Scott as the first president and CEO, then replaced Scott with himself from 1981 to 1983. In August 1978, the Continental Illinois National Bank and Trust Company invested $504,000.

On December 12, 1980, Apple went public, selling 4.6 million shares at $22 per share, generating over $100 million.

Other entrepreneurs start more modestly—but manage to grow. *Shark Tank* star Daymond John founded his clothing brand FUBU in his mother's house in Hollis, Queens. She taught him how to sew and supported him by allowing her house to be taken over to grow the business. In 1992, John and his mother mortgaged her house for $100,000 to generate startup capital. To fund a big order, they had to take out a second mortgage on the home. Then, a fortuitous investment from Samsung Textiles allowed them to complete their orders and get paid for them, starting a positive cash flow.

There are actually four owners of FUBU: Daymond John and his neighborhood friends Carlton E. Brown, J. Alexander Martin, and Keith C. Perrin. With hard work, the business took off: by 2017, FUBU had earned over $6 billion in global sales.

The advantages of being self-employed are numerous. You make the decisions and are responsible for the business's growth. You're likely to work seven days a week, at least in the early stages, and you won't make much money for yourself because you'll be plowing every spare dollar back into your dream, but if you succeed and your business flourishes, the rewards are generous. You'll have to become a jack of all trades because even if you hire specialists such as accountants or finance managers, you must know enough to determine if they're doing a good job.

Passive Income

The phrase, passive income, has a sweet ring to it and amounts to owning an asset that other people pay to use or rent, including stock or other securities that produce nice rates of return on investment. This makes you a part owner of an asset who shares in the profits. You can also create passive income by investing in or purchasing an entire business that operates without your day-to-day direct control.

Generally, the assets that provide massive passive income are real estate and stocks.

Consider, for example, the most successful real estate developer in the United States. His name is Donald—no, not *that* Donald, but a man in California named Donald Bren.

Born in Los Angeles, California, in 1932, Donald Bren earned a degree in economics and business administration from the University of Washington. After graduation, he served three years as an officer in the U.S. Marine Corps.

In 1958, at 26, Bren became a self-employed entrepreneur. He took out a $10,000 bank loan and built a house in Newport Beach. He sold the house and netted a small profit. After forming the Bren Company, he built and sold homes, reinvesting the profits in new developments. By the early 1960s, Bren had graduated to designing suburban master-planned communities. His largest project to date was a 10,000-acre city development in Mission Viejo, California.

Despite his success, Bren quickly realized the limitations of the build-and-sell business model. It worked, but selling houses provided no *passive income*. In 1977, in partnership with A. Alfred Taubman, a prominent shopping center developer, Bren bid $337.4 million to acquire the Irvine Company, the holding company that owned a sprawling 185-square-mile parcel known as Irvine Ranch. He then bought out Taubman's shares to become the sole owner. Since then, the Irvine Company has developed scores of residential and commercial properties.

As of 2022, the company's holdings comprised more than 560 office buildings, 125 apartment communities with 65,000 units, 40 retail centers, one coastal resort, three golf courses, and five marinas. Bren and his company own one-fifth of Orange County, an area five times the size of Manhattan. This includes the city of Irvine, largely designed by Bren himself. With a population of 250,000 and often referred to as the epicenter of Orange County, the city is home to residential villages, shopping centers, parks, top-ranked schools, and headquarters for more than one-third of the companies on the Fortune 500 list.

The company's investment property portfolio also includes assets in Silicon Valley, San Diego, West Los Angeles, Chicago, and New York City. All its properties produce a flow of passive income in the form of rents and lease payments.

With a net worth of $16.2 billion, Donald Bren was ranked number 112 on the 2022 Forbes Billionaires List.

In 2011, Bren told the *Los Angeles Times* he had learned a valuable lesson from his father: "When you hold property over the long term, you're able to create better values, and you have something tangible to show for it."

He didn't say this, but there was one caveat: You need to hold property over the long term, *which you rent or lease to others*. You own it, and they pay to use it. That's the winning formula!

As stated earlier, stock ownership can also provide massive passive income. Consider the heirs to the Wal-Mart retail empire built by family patriarch Sam Walton and his brother, Bud. Wal-Mart is the world's largest retailer, one of the world's largest business enterprises in terms of annual revenue, and, with just over 2.2 million employees, the world's largest private employer.

As of 2018, the Walton heirs own just under 50 percent of Wal-Mart's stock. The three most prominent living members—Sam's children Jim, Rob, and Alice Walton—have consistently been in the top 20 of the Forbes 400 list since 2001, as were John and Helen, who have both died. Christy Walton took her husband John's place in the ranking after his death. In 2020, the Walton estate, mostly in the form of Wal-Mart stock, was valued at $215 billion. The youngest brother, Jim Walton, is the wealthiest, with a reported net worth of $61 billion.

In September 2016, Jim Walton was reported to own over 152 million Wal-Mart shares worth over $11 billion. So why should he be worth $61 billion? This could be why:

1. Wal-Mart shares pay a dividend, so as long as you own them (and remember, Jim Walton paid *nothing* for them—he inherited them), you receive a passive income stream.

2. When you have a lot of money and provide it for other people to invest, they pay you for the privilege. In other words, you use your money to generate more money.

3. The more assets you own, the more money you can borrow from banks on the most favorable terms. You can use that money to make other investments, such as buying more real estate, and then pay off the loan and own the assets you bought with the borrowed money. In this way, you're using other people's money (OPM) to buy assets, which you then own and can use to make more money.

In short, the eternal rule of passive income is this: *The more money you have, the more money you can make just by using your money!*

How crazy is that? It's amazing!

Choose Your Road

You can enter the top tiers of the wealthy and get very rich on any one, or a combination, of these income-producing roads— employment, self-employment, or passive income.

Being employed as a paycheck worker is within reach of almost anyone with a decent level of health. It is the logical first step for those without a college education. Although minimum-wage jobs are the lowest rung on the workforce ladder, these starter positions can be a launchpad for more extraordinary things.

A majority of high-wage earners, business owners, and investors have a story or two about how they started out in a minimum-wage job and parlayed that job into the career they possess today. On-the-job experience can be a great asset when these experiences are converted into knowledge about properly handling people, money, and business matters.

These same on-the-job learning experiences can also be applied to running a small business if you choose that route. Before starting a small business, ask yourself a few pertinent questions: are you patient enough to endure all the government regulations and paperwork associated with the business sector you are looking to get into? Do you have a pleasing personality that prospects gravitate to, or are you standoffish and sometimes abrasive? These and other personal issues should be considered before opening any small business. If shortcomings exist, they can be overcome through education, personal development, or hiring out what you cannot manage properly.

If your management style doesn't allow employees to be on the payroll, choose a business you can operate as a sole proprietor. Many people do quite well as sole proprietors. You probably know a few of them.

Joseph Ades, also known as the "Gentleman Peeler," is a New York City legend who became a millionaire through the sole proprietor route. He was born in Manchester, England, in 1934, the youngest of seven children. Leaving school in 1949 at age 15, after a brief stint as an office boy, he became intrigued by the local markets that had sprung up in the war-torn cities of Northern England. He began hawking comic books before selling linens, textiles, jewelry, and toys directly on the streets.

He married and moved to Sydney, Australia, where he set up markets in the parking lots of drive-in movies. Eventually, he sold goods at street fairs off the back of a large truck.

Divorce followed, and then another marriage and another divorce. His career took its iconic direction after his third wife gave him a copy of *London Labour and the London Poor* by Henry Mayhew. Ades was fascinated by the street sellers whom Mayhew called "the patterers," many of whom adopted successful gentlemen's expensive dress and refined mannerisms. After the dissolution of his third marriage and a brief residence in Ireland, Ades followed his daughter to New York City.

There, at age 59, he reinvented his work life: he began a career as a sidewalk street vendor of five-dollar vegetable peelers. Every day, rain or shine, he would take his sales kit—boxes of Swiss-made stainless-steel peelers he had bought wholesale, a selection of vegetables and potatoes in four coolers, and a low stool—to a random street corner in Manhattan. Dressed in $1,000 Chester Barrie suits and shirts from Turnbull & Asser, he'd spend the day demonstrating his peeler and pattering in his charming British accent. Crowds would gather, and he'd sell peelers as quickly as he could stuff five-dollar bills into his pocket.

Joe Ades made enough money to enjoy café society at the Pierre Hotel on the Upper East Side and live with his fourth wife, Estelle Pascoe, in her three-bedroom apartment on Park Avenue. He put his granddaughters through college, and many people say he became a millionaire. He worked practically up until the day he died at age 75.

Mr. Ades, pronounced (Add-ess), owned a partnership in a real estate management firm, was a developer of malls and shopping centers, and possessed other passive income streams as well.

He is remembered for a pithy saying: "Never underestimate a small amount of money gathered by hand for 60 years."

Joe parlayed his business income into passive income streams. He made it, he saved it, then wisely invested it. You, too, can create passive income from earned, business income, or both. But first, you must be able to save a portion of all you earn.

Saving money comes naturally to some people, but with others, it is a learned skill. If you have issues with saving money but can see the benefits, an easy way to get started is to save one dollar a day, starting today. The idea of pulling a single dollar out of your pocket and using that dollar as a starting point for a savings account doesn't sound very promising, right? What if that single dollar became the basis of a lucrative change in your entire financial future?

A dollar-a-day savings is sufficient to begin a passive income savings that will eventually add up to some real money. Initially, it's more about conditioning your mind to the idea of saving. As you place that dollar into your savings each day, it quickly becomes a habit and something you look forward to funding. As the savings grow, you'll be intrigued by your newly discovered ability and begin exploring other ways of producing income to fund your savings. If you stay with it long enough, you'll see how a separate 100 dollar-a-month or more savings is possible.

It is eventually necessary to deposit your dollar-a-day savings into a separate bank account. Why? Because you don't want to mingle it with other savings and risk losing it. When your savings reach two thousand dollars, invest it into a low-risk investment account, typically containing mutual funds, with a registered broker with at least a ten-year track record of profitable investing.

Chapter 4

Find a Better Job

If you've read any of the hundreds of career books on the market, you'll know that 99 percent of them urge you to quit your boring corporate job and strike out on your own as an entrepreneur. The implication is that anyone who works for a company must be miserable and feel like a prisoner in a labor camp.

This is nonsense. As I've stated, millions of normal, smart, happy people thrive working within organizations. They derive great satisfaction from helping their team compete in the marketplace. In their 9–5 life, their purpose is to contribute to the company's success. They have no desire to jump off the big ship and get into a rowboat.

This chapter is called "Finding a Better Job." The premise is that you're happy in your chosen industry. It may be healthcare, manufacturing, hospitality, digital technology, retail, food service—you name it. You want to advance in your career by working a succession of jobs within your industry that offer higher pay and increasing responsibility, until you perhaps become CEO.

If you're *unhappy* in your current industry and you want to change careers, your path is very simple:

1. Get training. Earn the degree you need to qualify for your target job. But if you don't mind starting at the bottom, where you need only a high school diploma or GED, just start applying for jobs.

2. Be willing to take a pay cut. If you're making $150,000 a year as an advertising executive and want to become the director of a non-profit museum, be prepared to take half of your previous income until you can work your way up the ladder of the museum industry.

3. Sometimes, when you earn the necessary degree, you can change industries and immediately get paid more than you were previously. Bingo—you hit the jackpot!

You Can Be a "Lifer" Like These CEOs

Some people love working in a big organization and wouldn't want it any other way. Earlier in the book, I profiled Mary Barra, the remarkable chair and CEO of General Motors, who is a true "lifer," having started at GM at the age of 18 and slowly worked her way to the corner office.

If you find that you prefer to work within an organization, the following examples should be an inspiration to you. Here are a few:

Doug McMillion, President and CEO of Wal-Mart

In 1984, high school student Carl Douglas McMillon wanted to earn money to pay for college, so he took a job loading trucks at a Wal-Mart distribution center in Bentonville, Arkansas, which happened to be the company's global headquarters. At the time, he earned $6.50 an hour. He enjoyed working for Wal-Mart, and after earning his MBA, he rejoined the company as an assistant manager at a Tulsa, Oklahoma, store. He rose through the ranks, taking on titles including general merchandise manager and CEO of Sam's Club. In 2014, he was named president and CEO of Wal-Mart.

"Having been here a long time, I think I had the feeling that I knew what responsibility felt like," McMillon told *Fortune* in 2015. "And then you move into the role, and you find out there's a whole 'nother level of it."

Bob Iger, CEO of the Walt Disney Company

Sometimes, the path to the top has twists and turns because the company you start with may be acquired by another company—and you keep climbing the ladder.

In 1973, Robert Allen Iger started his career as a weatherman at a news station in Ithaca, New York. He then moved to New York City, where he repaired television sets for ABC before becoming a studio facility supervisor. He then moved on to ABC Sports and later to the head of programming at ABC. In 1994, Iger was named president and chief operating officer of ABC's corporate parent, Capital Cities/ABC.

The next year, the Walt Disney Co. purchased Capital Cities/ABC. Iger now had a taller ladder to climb! In 2005, Disney announced that Iger would succeed Michael Eisner as CEO, a position he held until he retired in 2021.

He wrote in his book *The Ride of a Lifetime: Lessons Learned from 15 Years as CEO of the Walt Disney Company*, "At its essence, good leadership isn't about being indispensable; it's about helping others be prepared to possibly step into your shoes—giving them access to your own decision making, identifying the skills they need to develop and helping them improve, and, as I've had to do, sometimes being honest with them about why they're not ready for the next step up."

Karen Kaplan, Chair and CEO of Hill Holliday

Hill Holliday (HH) is a marketing and communications agency based in Boston, Massachusetts, with offices in New York City and Greenville, South Carolina. The 17th largest advertising agency in the U.S., it's part of the world's third-largest advertising and marketing conglomerate, IPG.

In 1982, when she was 22 years old and a graduate of the University of Massachusetts with a BA in French language and literature, Karen Kaplan set her sights on attending law school. But she needed money, so she interviewed at Hill Holliday for the receptionist job. It's unclear whether she had any particular interest in advertising. She was hired—and she never left. Instead, she rose through the ranks at the marketing company, eventually holding 16 different positions. Three decades later, Kaplan was named CEO of Hill Holliday.

She has been named one of the "100 Most Influential Women in Advertising" by *Advertising Age*.

"I was going to be the best-damned receptionist in history, and that's how I approached the job," Kaplan told *Fortune* in 2014. "I took it really seriously. I didn't just bide my time out there."

Or You Can Leapfrog from Company to Company

The three previous examples are people who joined a company at a relatively young age and stayed with that same company for their entire career, eventually rising to the top.

Getting promoted from within is a relatively simple task. You're already working at the company, your employment history is an open book, and the interview process will likely be short. The company knows it can save money on headhunting and other onboarding costs, and if they promote you, you'll be able to hit the ground running.

But in reality, lifetime employment with one company is not the rule but the exception. It's more common for rising stars to leapfrog from one company to another because they find their way to the top blocked by the "seniority traffic jam"—that is, the competition from entrenched people above them who are either in place and not retiring or who are looking to advance and are virtually guaranteed priority promotions.

Getting a better job by leaving your current company and getting hired by a competitor is a much more complicated task that requires planning and a good strategy. Most importantly, the best strategy is one you implement long before you actually decide to look for a new job outside your company.

When You Have Friends in High Places

We know the easiest and most friction-free way to move up the ladder is by getting promoted within your company. This is because the person hiring you already knows your background and is comfortable with you. Giving you the job is a low-risk decision. The person hiring you could never be accused of making a bad hire because you already work at the company!

Therefore, we can easily conclude that the most compelling reason to hire someone is that they're a known quantity and the risk is low. Their resume is almost irrelevant. The interview process becomes a formality.

If already working at your company is the number one way to get hired for a more senior position, then what's the number two way?

The number two way is to be highly recommended by someone who works at your target company. This person would be a professional colleague with a personal relationship with you.

Here's a typical scenario. The Alpha Company knows that Bob is retiring as assistant vice president. The search for a replacement begins. Susan is on the search committee. She tells them she knows a terrific candidate, Phil, who works at Beta Company and is looking for a change. Phil would be perfect, she says. I've known him for years. He'll hit the ground running, and I know we'll work well together.

The committee trusts Susan and wants to make the process short and sweet. They say, "Okay, let's bring in Phil." They meet Phil and agree he's the person for the job.

Meanwhile, they've advertised the job, and they've received a pile of applications. Many of the candidates are terrible, but a few are qualified. For the sake of appearances, they bring in some of the candidates for interviews. They aren't going to hire any of them, but they interview them.

Sadly, sometimes, this is done so the company can claim to have met a diversity goal.

In June 2022, Wells Fargo found itself under federal criminal investigation over accusations that the company conducted sham job interviews with diverse candidates after positions had already been awarded to a chosen candidate. Women, people of color, and other diverse candidates reportedly were brought in for interviews for jobs they had no chance of winning.

It began in 2020 when Wells Fargo announced a policy requiring hiring managers to consider a diverse slate of candidates for high-paying jobs at the firm. The policy was similar to the National Football League's so-called Rooney Rule, named for Dan Rooney, a former owner of the Pittsburgh Steelers. The rule was devised after researchers demonstrated to league officials that Black coaches were not being interviewed for top positions. The Rooney Rule required the teams in the league to interview at least one non-white candidate for any senior role like head coach or general manager.

In early 2022, a group of Black coaches sued the NFL, claiming they were subject to bogus interviews. They asserted that the organizations had no intention of hiring them—it was all for show.

As for Wells Fargo, according to *The New York Times*, inside sources at the bank described the phony interview process as a "checkbox effort" that would create an audit record for regulators showing that Wells Fargo considered a diverse range of candidates without actually making a meaningful effort to diversify the workforce.[7]

In any case, these issues should not deter you from trying to position yourself as favorably as possible in your job market. The reality is that if you are already known to the person or committee doing the hiring and have a good reputation, you

---

[7] NYT. https://www.nytimes.com/2022/05/19/business/wells-fargo-fake-interviews.html

will have a better chance of being hired than someone coming in off the street.

To make yourself known and build up your circle of contacts in your industry, you need to network relentlessly.

Networking

The end goal of any networking activity is to make your persona and abilities well known so that your industry contacts will perceive you as a valuable asset to their organization.

While you can do this virtually, which I'll discuss, the best way is to get to know people in your industry personally. Meet, see, and hang out with them face to face.

How can you do this?

There are two resources you need to tap.

Family and School Associations

You may know people from your past who occupy influential positions. Get out there and show your face.

The most obvious are two groups of people.

1. Your parents' friends. Countless young people have been launched into their careers because their mom or dad—or even aunt or uncle—made a phone call to a friend and said, "My kid is looking for a job. How about giving him a try?" The

person hires *you* because they know your mom or dad. If you have such connections, be shameless. Leverage them!

2. Former classmates. School connections are very powerful—especially college connections and, most of all, Greek letter society connections. Sororities, fraternities, and secret societies exist primarily to forge bonds of unity and trust between their members that will last a lifetime. At elite universities, secret societies are like fraternities on steroids. For example, at Yale University, the Skull and Bones secret society of fourth-year undergrads boasts three "Bonesmen" who have become president of the United States: William Howard Taft, George H. W. Bush, and George W. Bush. We don't know who the Bonesmen are—the list is secret—but you can be sure *they* know who they are!

These family and school connections can be very valuable. Maintain them, and don't hesitate to use them.

Trade Association and Civic Association Colleagues

Most industries have trade associations that have regular meetings or conferences in which people who are normally competitors come together to discuss issues affecting their industry. Many are local and really big ones that attract attendees worldwide. For example, in the technology industry, here are just a few major conferences:

Digital Workplace Experience: A four-part virtual event series that gathers over 500 leading digital workplace thinkers under one roof.

Deep Learning Summit, San Francisco, CA: Brings together the latest technologies and leaders in AI to solve business and societal challenges.

Share Dallas, Dallas, TX: Hands-on sessions focused on IT hot topics like cloud technology, mainframe hardware, security, and more.

EmTech Digital, Cambridge, MA: A signature event on business leadership and artificial intelligence.

Microsoft Ignite: Microsoft's annual virtual gathering of technology leaders and practitioners from across the globe. It's huge, with over 1,000 sessions.

Think Digital Event Experience: The annual IBM business and technology conference.

Augmented World Expo USA, Santa Clara, CA: The world's premiere AR+VR conference and expo.

Pure//Accelerate: One of the most sought-after technological events in the world.

Cisco Live, Las Vegas, NV: A premier education and training event for IT professionals.

Digital Enterprise Show, Málaga, Spain: A global expo and congress dedicated to digital transformation.

Dublin Tech Summit, Dublin, Ireland: A one-day global technology conference bringing together influential leaders in business and technology.

The Next Web Conference, Amsterdam, Netherlands: Brings people together for interactive sessions, keynotes, and intimate one-on-one conversions.

Design Thinking & Innovation Week, London, UK: A feature-packed conference for creative entrepreneurs, innovation directors, and business owners.

UX and Digital Design Week, London, UK: An immersive five-day experience with talks, round tables, studio visits, and mini workshops from the most influential digital companies in the world.

Technology & Innovation, Austin, TX: A three-day event that covers the full scope of technology options available to marketing and sales professionals.

IT Arena, Lviv, Ukraine: A three-day conference filled with ground-breaking solutions and forward-thinking business ideas that inspire exponential growth in those who attend. This conference is where you meet global changemakers and the most inspiring tinkerers while learning revolutionary modernizations that transform the tech space.

TechCrunch Disrupt, San Francisco, CA: A unique and innovative conference where the startup world gathers to see the present and future of tech under one roof.

There are many more, both in tech and every major industry and many niche industries.

If the business travel industry is your chosen career path, then you'll want to attend the annual convention of the Global

Business Travel Association (GBTA). The association's membership includes more than 9,000 business travel professionals worldwide, including global business travel and meeting planners, as well as suppliers across the global travel industry marketplace.

Or maybe you're working in the recreational boating industry? Then you'll want to check out the Elevate Summit in Orlando, FL, which describes itself as an intimate gathering of thought leaders who come to focus on, address, and learn the latest developments regarding key issues impacting the recreational boating industry and their business. Organizers say one of the key benefits of attending is to meet new colleagues and industry leaders and learn from top marine industry experts.

There are thousands of such organizations—just search for the ones representing your industry, whether in your area or nationally.

Local Business Organizations

Don't forget the traditional local business groups, including the Rotary Club and the Chamber of Commerce. While these organizations have members from many industries, they're big enough to include representatives from all the local businesses in one industry. For example, if you're in banking, you'll rub shoulders with many other banking professionals from other local banks or bank branches.

If your primary goal in business networking is to gain many referrals, Business Networking International (BNI) may be a valuable resource. BNI calls itself the world's leading business referral organization, with over 286,000 members and 10,600 chapters available worldwide.

LinkedIn has emerged as a potent networking forum. While having a robust LinkedIn profile can be useful in promoting yourself and your business, LinkedIn also has numerous groups based on business interests and location. Joining one or more of these groups can help you connect with others in your field and community. Some of these groups exist for the sole purpose of networking across all industries within a region. Many hold public events, which can be a great way to rub shoulders and connect with others face-to-face.

Network After Work is a professional community of business professionals dedicated to developing relationships to grow their businesses and careers. Members can create online profiles, search for other members within the same field or location and attend virtual and in-person events. The organization also hosts live events in locations across the United States.

Both Eventbrite and Meetup are online directories where you can connect with various activities, from business networking events to music festivals and creative adventures.

By the way, these organizations are valuable not just for people who work for businesses large or small but for entrepreneurs launching their own businesses.

Your LinkedIn Profile

In addition to meeting people in person and networking with them, just about everyone has an online presence. Most professionals maintain an account on LinkedIn. Facebook is more for personal and family stuff. TikTok is mostly used for entertainment, and Instagram really isn't relevant for career content. Twitter and a few other social media startups are worth looking at, but you must judge whether they are right for you.

Your online presence on any platform must be professional and career focused. Don't post photos of you and your buddies getting drunk in Cancun. Avoid overt political talk. Keep your clothes on and under *no circumstances* post anything you wouldn't want a hiring manager to see. Companies view your social media presence as an extension of your business life. And if you work for them—or hope to work for them—they'll tell you that your online presence reflects upon the company. In the online world, everything is public information.

On the resume portion of your LinkedIn profile, go the extra mile and don't simply state your job responsibilities. Present an interesting story about your successes on the job. Highlight a problem and how you solved it, especially if you came up with a creative solution. Keep your narrative succinct; a lengthy yarn could turn off busy recruiters.

Take this advice from the CEO of LinkedIn, Jeff Weiner: "Be yourself, represent who you are. It's not just your experiences; this is not a resume. This is a more dynamic approach to representing your experiences, your skills, your objectives, what you know, and what you're interested in within a professional context. It's not just about the comprehensiveness; it's also about the freshness of the information, and the more complete and the fresher, the more opportunities that will accrue to our members."[8]

One feature of LinkedIn is that you can message hiring managers directly. It's important that in your initial message, you simply introduce yourself and aren't pushy. You want the executive to see your credentials on LinkedIn and remember who you are. Try to find some common ground in your message. Mention the people you know in common and compliment their personality and professionalism.

Like millions of other professionals, you can have a great life working for a company as an employee. If that brings you happiness and fulfillment, by all means, go for

---

[8] CBS News. https://www.cbsnews.com/news/linkedin-ceo-jeff-weiner-on-microsoft-acquisition-management-style-and-the-perfect-profile/

Chapter 5

Self-Employment: Start Your Own Business

Many people dream of becoming independent business owners and end up having their dreams shot down by their negative pre-programming. Listening to the irrational fears that pop into your mind will cause your aspirations to come crashing down and pull you back into the same rut that led you to those thoughts of more time freedom in the first place.

Then there are people—perhaps you—who can block out all the negativity as if they have blinders on. These people are their own boss and live by the terms they set. Their business defines who they are, and their service is a way of making a meaningful impact on the world.

Such a person is an entrepreneur. He or she creates a new business, bearing most risks while reaping the rewards. The entrepreneur is commonly seen as an innovator, a source of new ideas, goods, services, and procedures. After all, it would be pointless to launch a business that perfectly duplicates what some local existing business does; you've got to put your own spin on it, even if you're selling a commodity like pizza.

Entrepreneurs come in all shapes and sizes.

Some, like Bill Gates, start at a young age. He was 20 years old when he left Harvard to launch Microsoft. His fellow Harvard dropout, Mark Zuckerberg, was 21 when he quit school to launch Facebook. Many entrepreneurs show their spirit when they're kids. After trying to sell Christmas trees and parakeets, Sir Richard Branson's first successful business venture, at the age of 18, was a magazine called *Student*. Then, he set up a mail-order record business, followed by a chain of record stores known as Virgin Records. He has dyslexia, was never a "team player," and had poor grades; on his last day at Stowe School, his headmaster, Robert Drayson, told him he would either become a millionaire or end up in prison.

Others become entrepreneurs when they have an irresistible idea. Sara Blakely, who founded Spanx at 27, was previously a corporate employee; she worked for the office supply company Danka, selling fax machines door to door. She was good at sales and was promoted to national sales trainer at 25. If her uncomfortable pantyhose hadn't bothered her, she might have stayed with the company!

Some people take a while to strike out on their own. Born in 1890, Harlan David Sanders worked various ordinary paycheck jobs—many of which he got fired from—before starting to sell fried chicken from a gas station restaurant during the Great Depression. In 1935, in recognition of his exceptional fried chicken recipe, Kentucky governor Ruby

Laffoon commissioned Sanders as an honorary Kentucky colonel, thereby making him "Colonel Sanders."

The Second World War disrupted his fledgling business, and after working various dead-end jobs, in 1952, when he was 62 years old, Colonel Sanders franchised his secret "Kentucky Fried Chicken" recipe to Pete Harman of South Salt Lake, Utah, the owner of one of that city's largest restaurants. Sanders liked the idea, and in the late 1950s, he pursued the franchise model aggressively, driving from city to city looking for partners. Finally, in 1964, at 73, he sold the entire Kentucky Fried Chicken corporation for $2 million ($17.5 million today) and became its salaried "brand ambassador."

His success took a long time—but eventually, Colonel Sanders made his fortune!

Market Need + New Idea + Determination = Success

One of the greatest debates of entrepreneurship is this: Should you figure out what the market needs and then develop a product or service to fill that need, or invent an innovative new gadget or service and then build a business around it?

To be honest, the answer is you need to do both.

Generally, whether your startup company is business-to-business (B2B) or business-to-consumer (B2C), you need to hit that sweet spot where you're filling a need in the marketplace with a product or service that's both innovative and effective.

For example, in the B2B space, look at Salesforce, the cloud computing company with a 2022 market valuation of $58 billion. Salesforce was founded in 1999 by Marc Benioff and three partners. (To launch Salesforce, Benioff quit his job as vice president of the mighty database company Oracle after working his way up from customer support over 13 years.)

Their idea was twofold. First, to make customer relationship management (CRM) easier and cheaper for corporate customers by providing CRM software and applications focused on sales, customer service, marketing automation, analytics, and application development. None of these were novel ideas. What set Salesforce apart was the second idea: Benioff's vision of these services being delivered via the cloud. Salesforce offered a single product—a CRM software tool—based on a new marketing concept. Instead of buying and installing the software on individual computers, Salesforce offered their product through the cloud. They wouldn't buy or install software from a physical disk or CD. Instead, they'd access the service over the internet from a central facility. Cloud-based services are universally accepted now, but in 1999, this was a crazy idea!

To make it super-simple to operate, Salesforce's CRM software would be extremely user-friendly, affordable, easy to set up, integrate with existing software platforms, and run faster than lightning, as the company promised.

The idea was mocked by software industry elitists who failed to recognize the threat Salesforce represented against the big software providers. *Business Insider* wrote an early story about Salesforce entitled "The Ant at the Picnic." Salesforce was up against software heavyweights Oracle and Siebel, who were making billions of dollars selling enterprise software that had to be installed and updated on the client's network. Their installed software provided the same type of solution as Salesforce's inexpensive web-based solution, but the Salesforce idea to deliver their services online made it infinitely simpler, with no requirement that the customer endure updates because those happened automatically on the Salesforce servers.

Benioff, his partners, and their investors saw that their product worked. They knew if they persisted, the corporate world would eventually come around. In 2004—after just five years in business—Salesforce announced its IPO. On the first day of trading, the company made headlines as its stock gained over 55 percent appreciation. It was a testament to how Salesforce had built a product people loved, continued growing, and successfully started selling people on their vision for the cloud.

To recap, the success of Salesforce, like every other entrepreneurial idea, was based on three things:

1. A need in the marketplace.

2. A new innovation that could solve that need.

3. The unflinching determination of the founders and investors to succeed.

Sometimes, the invention comes first, and a business follows. You might say this happened with the personal computer pioneered by Steve Jobs and Steve Wozniak. Undoubtedly, the invention—a computer anyone could use—was cool. But what could average people do with it, aside from using it as a glorified typewriter or to play video games? In 1976, Jobs looked for investments to expand the fledgling business, but banks refused to lend him money because the idea of a computer for ordinary people seemed absurd at the time.

For his part, Jobs seemed to suggest that the customer would figure out what they could do with a personal computer, which would inform the design evolution.

"Technology is nothing," he said. "What's important is that you have faith in people, that they're basically good and smart—and if you give them tools, they'll do wonderful things with them. Tools are just tools. They either work, or they don't work."[9]

The Pet Rock

If you've ever watched the TV show *Shark Tank*, you'll know that the Sharks frequently say to the prospective

---

[9] CNBC.com. https://www.cnbc.com/2019/10/05/apple-ceo-steve-jobs-technology-is-nothing-heres-what-it-takes-to-achieve-great-success.html

entrepreneur, "You've got a product, but you don't have a business."

What does this mean?

It means that while your product may be innovative or marketable, the Sharks don't see how it could sustain a long-term business that can keep growing. That is to say, having a quirky new gizmo might get you some sales in the short term, but after a while, it will hit its peak and then decline—and so will your income.

A classic example of this is the Pet Rock.

In the spring of 1975, Gary Dahl worked as a freelance advertising copywriter in California. While having drinks at a bar with friends, the conversation turned to the fact that pets were high maintenance. Dogs and cats required constant attention, from walking to feeding to cleaning up after them.

Dahl laughed and quipped that he didn't have to worry about any of that because he had a "pet rock."

Dahl received a round of laughter but saw potential and began working on the idea. The product wouldn't be just the rocks, which were ordinary stones from Mexico's Rosarito Beach, but humorous packaging as well. He wrote an owner's manual for the pet rock, including how to care for it, the tricks it could perform ("play dead" being the most obvious), and how it could remain a faithful companion due to its "long life span." He designed a cardboard box with excelsior padding and air holes for the imaginary pet. As a helpful cultural echo, it resembled a McDonald's Happy Meal container.

Dahl recruited two colleagues, George Coakley and John Heagerty, to invest. They both agreed, with Coakley investing $10,000—roughly $60,000 in 2022 dollars.

In August 1975, Dahl launched the Pet Rock at a gift show in San Francisco. The retail price for the Pet Rock was just $4.00—very affordable. The response was immediate. Neiman Marcus ordered 1,000 rocks. Bloomingdale's took it also. *Newsweek* did a story with a picture. Dahl had a full-blown fad on his hands.

The fad lasted six months, with a blizzard of sales during the 1975 Christmas season, during which Dahl was selling them as fast as he could make them. By February 1976, sales had dried up and the product vanished from the public's consciousness—but not before Dahl had sold 1.5 million Pet Rocks and became a millionaire with his profit of nearly a dollar a rock.[10]

Gary Dahl was lucky: he knew he had a fad that wouldn't last long. He tried to launch a few other novelty items, but they flopped, and he quickly abandoned them. The Pet Rock was never a *business*. Dahl enjoyed the roller-coaster ride while it lasted, and then he got off.

---

[10] https://www.mercurynews.com/2015/04/01/the-story-of-gary-dahl-and-the-pet-rock-from-the-archives/

But is it possible to build a business from "fad" products?

Yes, it is.

Wham-O Succeeds as a Business

In 1948, Richard Knerr and Arthur "Spud" Melin were two University of Southern California graduates who were miserable with their paycheck jobs and decided to start their own business. In the Knerr family garage in South Pasadena, they developed their first product, a powerful slingshot. They called their fledgling operation the Wham-O Manufacturing Company, and they marketed the Wham-O Slingshot.

It wasn't a gag gift like the Pet Rock; the slingshot was adopted by clubs for competitive target shooting and small game hunting. But it was just a slingshot, and you can sell only so many slingshots. The Pet Rock was a popular fad but not a viable long term business. Still, Knerr and Melin were determined to make Wham-O a prosperous corporation. To do that, they needed a steady pipeline of successful products with sustained sales and positive cash flow.

Their next product came from an unlikely source. For thousands of years, indigenous people have used hoops made of willow or bamboo in ceremonial dances. In 1957, Knerr and Melin manufactured a version in colorful plastic and called their new product the Hula-Hoop. It became the biggest toy fad in modern history, with 25 million sold in just four months. In two years, sales reached more than 100 million. The craze lasted until the end of 1959 and netted Wham-O $45 million. They still sell steadily today.

Two years after the Hula-Hoop, the company had another huge success with the Frisbee, which they had bought from inventor Fred Morrison.

In the early 1960s came the Super Ball, a high-bouncing ball made of a hard elastomer polybutadiene alloy dubbed Zectron. The material was invented by chemist Norman Stingley, who sold it to Wham-O. But the product itself needed development.

"It took us nearly two years to iron the kinks out of Super Ball before we produced it," said Knerr in 1966. "It always had that marvelous springiness, but it tended to fly apart. We've licked that with a very high-pressure technique for forming it. Now we're selling millions."[11]

Around 20 million Super Balls were sold that decade.

Over the years, Knerr and Melin relentlessly searched for new products. Many of them were flops. But enough of them were hits, including Silly String, Magic Sand, the Hacky Sack, the Boogie Board, and the EZ Spin Foam Frisbee Disk.

Today, Wham-O is a privately held company headquartered in Los Angeles, California. It does not release financial information and estimates of its annual revenues vary wildly.

---

[11] Griswald, Wesley S. (January 1966). "Can You Invent a Million-Dollar Fad?" *Popular Science*. 188 (1): 78–81.

Lessons from Wham-O (and Others)

As an aspiring entrepreneur, what can you learn from a company that got its start selling slingshots, Hula-Hoops, and Frisbees?

Plenty. Here are a few lessons that apply to every successful entrepreneur:

1. Be relentlessly focused on success. Their products may have been lighthearted, but Knerr and Melin were very serious about their business. They have that determined mindset in common with Thomas Edison, Henry Ford, Steve Jobs, Bill Gates, and every other successful entrepreneur who began in a garage or small workshop. When you're working for yourself, failure is not an option. You must figure out a way to succeed, or you *may* starve.

When Jeff Bezos left his high-paying Wall Street job in 1993 and relocated to his family's garage in Bellevue, Washington, to launch his internet bookstore, many of his friends and family had big doubts.

Why did he do it?

He has spoken about his "regret minimization framework." That is to say, he had a hunch that the internet could be a powerful tool for selling everyday items, and he didn't want to reach old age and regret not taking the plunge.

Investors who shared his vision were hard to find. In 1994, Bezos held 60 meetings with family members, friends, and prospective investors to convince them to each invest $50,000 in Amazon and help him raise $1 million. Only 20 said yes, including his mother and stepfather, who invested $245,573 in the new venture. His mother, Jackie, warned, "Don't quit your job. Can you do this on the weekends and nights?" His stepfather, Mike, reportedly asked his stepson, "What's the internet?"[12]

Bezos knew it was risky; he warned many early investors that there was a 70 percent chance that Amazon would fail or go bankrupt. In the fourth quarter of 2001, the company finally turned its first profit—and the rest is history.

2. You don't need to be an inventor. Knerr and Melin didn't invent the slingshot, Hula-Hoop, Frisbee, Super Ball, or any other product they sold. What set them apart is that they recognized the *potential* in products other people had invented and developed those products to sell to a mass market. They knew what the product needed to become profitable, and they took the time and work necessary to achieve their goal. For example, when Norman Stingley invented his polybutadiene synthetic rubber ball, he first offered it to his employer, the Bettis Rubber Company. The company rejected it because the material was not very durable. Stingley then approached Knerr and Melin, who said, "We're going to make this work." It took

---

[12] CNBC.com. https://www.cnbc.com/2018/08/02/how-jeff-bezos-got-his-parents-to-invest-in-amazon--turning-them-into.html

them two years of developing and testing, but the effort paid off.

Jeff Bezos didn't invent the internet, and he didn't invent the bookstore. He didn't even invent online retailing. English entrepreneur Michael Aldrich was a pioneer of online shopping as early as 1979. In 1982, a company called Boston Computer Exchange launched an online marketplace for used computers, and in 1992, Book Stacks Unlimited opened an online bookstore.

So, how did Jeff Bezos prevail? He took these fragmentary ideas that other people had not fully or properly exploited and put them together, bigger and better.

This is the number one rule of entrepreneurship. This is what Sam Walton, Sir Richard Branson, Michael Dell, and all the rest did. They did it bigger and better than the other guy.

Do you think Thomas Edison invented the light bulb? He did not. The basic technology was well-known, and other inventors had made working light bulbs before Edison. But Edison solved the most vexing problem: Making a filament that would last without burning out. Edison claimed, "Before I got through, I tested no fewer than 6,000 vegetable growths and ransacked the world for the most suitable filament material." His innovation made the electric light both practical and marketable.

3. Keep your product pipeline full. You must always have something to sell that people want to buy. If you sell products that are *consumed*, like pizza or shampoo, you can frequently sell the same product to the same person. Likewise, selling a service that a customer can use repeatedly is good, also. Repeat customers are the holy grail of any business.

But if, like Wham-O, you sell durable products that are unlikely to be purchased repeatedly by the same customer, then you need a steady flow of *new* products for your customer to buy. A person is unlikely to buy more than one Super Ball, but they might buy a Super Ball, a Frisbee, a Hula-Hoop, and so on.

In the world of consumer goods manufacturing, Alfred P. Sloan was a pioneer in consumer stimulation. He was the CEO of General Motors in the 1920s. At that time, Ford ruled the auto market, and Henry Ford took pride in that his flagship product, the Model T, did *not* change much from year to year. There were minor improvements, but if your Model T was five years old, it was hard to distinguish it from a new one.

Sloan thought Ford was leaving money on the table. Why not convince the owner of the perfectly good five-year-old vehicle that it was time for an upgrade? To prod current GM owners to trade in their old cars for new ones, he invented the concept of the annual model change. For example, the 1928 Buick would be different enough from the 1927 Buick to be noticeable to the customer and his neighbors.

"The changes in the new model should be so novel and attractive as to create demand," wrote Sloan in his 1963 autobiography *My Years with General Motors*, "and a certain amount of dissatisfaction with past models as compared with the new one." Soon, this strategy of introducing products with *planned obsolescence* would become a key part of the American and global consumer economy.

Bernard London coined the term in his 1932 essay, "Ending the Depression through Planned Obsolescence." He stated that the government should impose a certain planned obsolescence on products so customers would keep coming back and buying more, therefore pulling the economy out of the Great Depression.

As industrial designer Brooks Stevens said in 1954, "Instill in the buyer the desire to own something a little newer, a little better, a little sooner than is necessary."[13]

Today, the undisputed champion of planned obsolescence is Apple. The company's seemingly endless software updates frustrate many customers but keep the cash flowing into the company. From the company's point of view, if you rule the market and nearly everyone owns your product, then if you want to keep earning revenue, you need to find a way to entice or force your customers to buy the newer model.

4. Be realistic about your products and your market. Very few products are "evergreen"—meaning they sell consistently year after year. Nearly every product must be regularly refreshed or improved, or else it needs to be phased out. Richard Knerr

---

[13] https://timeline.com/gm-invented-planned-obsolescence-cc19f207e842

said about the Super Ball, "Each Super Ball bounce is 92 percent as high as the last. If our sales don't come down any faster than that, we've got it made."[14] He meant that he knew the Super Ball would peak in sales and then slowly decline. Unlike the Pet Rock, which declined to zero, the Super Ball and many other Wham-O products declined to a base level of sales, which then stayed consistent for decades. When that happens, the company must ask itself, "Are we still making a profit at a lower level of sales? Is there anything we can do to revitalize sales?" If the answer to either question is "yes," there's reason enough to keep producing it.

5. Differentiate your brand from the crowd. The consumer must have a reason for buying your product or service rather than your competitor's. Many brands have collapsed because they have no distinct identity. This is particularly common with retailers. In recent years, prominent bankruptcies have included Olympia Sports, Stein Mart, Lord & Taylor, Brooks Brothers, JCPenney, Neiman Marcus, J. Crew, Pier 1 Imports, Barney's New York, Payless, Sears, Brookstone, the list is long. A company like Wham-O stands out by its relentless focus on its core image: Fun, inexpensive toys that anyone can enjoy. Wham-O does not make complicated or expensive toys. They stick to what they know.

---

[14] Hoffmann, Frank W.; William G. Bailey (1994). *Fashion & Merchandising Fads.* Routledge. pp. 243–244. ISBN 1-56024-376-7.

The Bottom Line

If you want to strike out on your own, know one thing: There's no formula for your success. Your situation is unique. There's no other company exactly like yours. Contradictions will abound. You need good advice, but you also need to ignore naysayers. You must keep ownership of your business while possibly giving up parts of it to your investors. You must keep the cash flow coming while looking for funds to fill your orders. You need to hire employees and give them autonomy while staying in control. You need to stand out in the marketplace while seeming familiar enough so that consumers trust you.

And above all, if you want to succeed, you must never be deterred by frequent failures. Learn from them and keep going.

Chapter 6

Build Passive Income

Asset ownership is the secret ingredient to mega-wealth.

Regardless of whether you choose to climb the ladder to become CEO of a company or break out on your own as an entrepreneur, to build truly significant wealth, you must step up into the class of people who own an asset that produces income without any effort from the owner.

If you're an employee or an entrepreneur, your income is directly tied to your work hours. You get paid for working and producing wealth for the company's owners unless the company's owner happens to be you.

If you stop working for any reason, your income will cease. If you're laid off through no fault of your own, you *may* get a severance payment. Then, you *might* be eligible to collect state unemployment insurance. When that runs out, you'll be living on hope and a prayer. When you retire, you may have your retirement account and Social Security, but those income streams are limited. Even if you have these various safety nets, when you stop working, your income will drop.

Without passive income, you're no better off than a cab driver collecting his fares. As long as you're behind the wheel of your cab, taking passengers from point A to point B, you can make money, but when you park the cab for the last time, you're not collecting any more fares.

So, how can you break free from the hamster wheel of earned income?

There are three ways.

The first is to create a product from which you collect a royalty for every unit sold. You can collect royalties on consumer products as well as works of reproducible media such as books and popular music.

The second is to have a significant ownership stake in an asset that produces a profit by selling something—that is, by owning stock in a company.

The third is to have an ownership stake in an asset that people will pay to use for some time. They may use the asset and even have control over it, but they will not *own* it. You will. Typically, this asset is real estate.

Royalties

In 1965, a team of scientists working in a lab at the University of Florida invented a sports drink specially designed for athletes. Its name, "Gatorade," was derived from the nickname of the university's sports teams. Ownership of the drink was offered to Stokely Van-Camp, who agreed to pay the scientists $25,000 upfront, a $5,000 bonus, and—this is the important part—a royalty of five cents on every gallon sold. In May 1967, a trust was formed called the Gatorade Trust, which originally had nine members, including doctors, two trainers, and a lab technician. The royalties due to the inventors of Gatorade were paid into the trust for disbursement to the nine members.

Fifty years later, in October 2015, it was announced that the sum of royalties paid to the Gatorade Trust had exceeded $1 billion.

"Things really took off when Quaker Oats bought the brand in 1983," said Dr. Jim Free, one of the inventors and a beneficiary of the trust. "They really knew how to connect it to what was going on on the field and had all the deals with the major sports."[15]

Now, that's passive income!

Other examples of passive royalty income include:

- Authors of books. Traditionally, authors earn 10 percent royalties on each book they sell. In 2021, the world's highest-paid authors included J. K. Rowling (net worth $1 billion), James Patterson ($800 million), and Stephen King ($500 million). As long as their books sell, the checks keep coming. As a side note,

---

[15] ESPN. https://www.espn.com/college-football/story/_/id/13789009/royalties-gatorade-inventors-surpass-1-billion

don't overlook self-publishing, it is also creating many millionaires these days.

- Musicians. They include Rihanna ($1.4 billion), Jay-Z ($1.4 billion), Paul McCartney ($1.28 billion), and Andrew Lloyd Webber (1.2 billion). For many, including Rhianna, their royalty income is boosted by other business ventures, which they could undertake because they had a surplus of money.

- Film and TV people. Successful media properties often have income streams that last for decades in syndication or re-runs. For example, as of 2021, *Seinfeld* is considered the most successful second-run syndicated show of all time. Since NBC aired the last episode in 1998, it's generated over $3.1 billion in syndication fees. Jerry Seinfeld himself has earned an estimated $400 million from syndication alone. The checks keep coming to his mailbox without Jerry lifting a finger.

The *Law & Order* TV drama series franchise is huge; creator Dick Wolf has earned over $830 million from the first-run episodes and the re-runs that constantly air in nearly every market. It's estimated that every hour of every day, he earns about $20,000 in royalties. That's $333 every minute, whether he's working, sleeping, eating, or just going for a walk.[16]

---

[16] https://www.celebritynetworth.com/richest-businessmen/producers/dick-wolf-net-worth/

You can buy royalty-producing assets. For example, in December 2020, Bob Dylan sold his entire catalog of songs to the Universal Music Publishing Group. The price was estimated at more than $300 million. His catalog includes more than 600 songs recorded thousands of times by other artists (generating royalties) and used in commercials and films (more royalties). Universal is betting that Dylan's songs will earn back the company's investment and a handsome profit in the next decade or so.

Stock Ownership

When you own stock, you're a part owner of a corporation whose intent is to provide a profit for its shareholders.

This happens in two ways.

The first way is that the value of the stock appreciates over time, and you'll hopefully net a profit when you sell it. Selling stock is similar to buying and selling any other asset—a house, a work of art, or a piece of jewelry. Once it's sold, it's gone. If you want to keep making money, you need to find another asset to buy at a low price and sell at a higher price.

The process can be time-consuming and is much like working a job unless you're operating at an elevated financial level with the assistance of a financial advisor or broker.

The second way is if the stock pays a dividend. These are usually small payments, but over time, they add up. Some companies pay paltry dividends that can't even match the inflation rate, while others are more robust. "Blue chip" companies known as strong dividend stocks include AT&T, Chevron, Xerox, IBM, and Altria Group. The thing about stock is that you normally need to own a lot of it to make any real money.

Many people who enjoy passive income and can live off it can do so because they own real estate. By real estate, I mean properties you own and hold for a long time and rent or lease to other people.

To make a sizable income from an asset you own that another person will pay to use, the asset itself needs to be significant and durable. It also needs to appreciate over the years, not depreciate.

Real estate fits the bill.

Single-Family Houses

Let's start with the most basic investment: single-family houses. These are generally considered poor investments if you want to generate income by renting them. This is because there's one caveat about real estate providing "passive" income: it's not entirely passive. Houses are complex physical structures. They have heating and cooling systems, electrical systems, plumbing systems, roofs, walls, and other features that can either wear out or be damaged by tenants. They require maintenance, and someone has to do it. If you do it yourself, you're working. You may enjoy this—but the rental income is not exactly passive.

Another issue with single-family homes is that, unlike multi-unit properties that contribute more than one source of income, if your single-family home is vacant, you have zero income but are still paying the mortgage and taxes. This is what is called a negative cash flow.

But like many things in business, these problems can be solved by going bigger.

Owning 10 or 20 single-family homes is different because now you can hire a manager to maintain them. You can get a blanket mortgage often used by investors, commercial property owners, and multi-family buyers looking to rent or use their properties for income. Investors often use blanket mortgages to either finance the purchase of multiple properties at once or consolidate their existing mortgages into a single, easy-to-manage loan.

If you have enough cash, which many institutional investors have, you can skip the mortgage altogether and pay in full upfront, which makes for a higher (ROI) return on your investment.

While single-family houses have traditionally been viewed as non-productive investments, since just before the Covid-19 pandemic, we've seen a big shift in institutional investing. Before that time, the single-family rental market was ignored by big institutional investors, who preferred multi-family properties. But big financiers like Blackstone, J.P. Morgan Asset Management, and Goldman Sachs Asset Management have bankrolled a growing industry of single-family home-rental companies that are both snapping up existing properties and building new ones. The biggest ones are publicly traded companies, including Invitation Homes, American Homes 4 Rent, and Tricon Residential—each owning tens of thousands of single-family rental homes.

As reported by Toptal.com, residential real estate acquired by companies or institutions soared to 90,215 homes in the third quarter of 2021, as investors, both large and small, accounted for 18 percent of single-family home sales. According to the online real estate firm Redfin, that's a whopping 80.2 percent increase from the previous year. Why is this happening? Finance writer Hudson Cashdan offered an interesting explanation—the emergence of Big Data: "The dramatic increase in computing power is enabling these new home-rental firms to scale and manage their portfolios more efficiently, not only enhancing the ability to analyze the market, speed up research, and make smart decisions more quickly, but also streamlining costs associated with property management. This convergence of market conditions and increased analytic power means these investors are likely here to stay."[17]

---

[17] Toptal.com. https://www.toptal.com/finance/real-estate/wall-street-buying-single-family-homes

Because they were more difficult to scale, single-family rentals were traditionally classified as "non-core," along with other specialty properties such as data centers, medical offices, hotels, and senior housing. But thanks to artificial intelligence and Big Data, that's no longer the case. Big companies can get nearly the same return on portfolios of single-family homes as they traditionally have made with multi-family apartments.

Multi-Family Structures

Many people have made fortunes investing in and managing multi-family properties. Multi-family housing provides affordable units, particularly in high-cost housing markets. By grouping many units under one roof, you reduce your expenses while increasing your rental income. And when you hire a management company, your property becomes a passive income source. You can literally lie on the beach in Jamaica and, with your cell phone, keep tabs on your properties.

Multi-family structures are classified in a variety of ways. One way is by the number of units and how they're arranged. Multi-family housing types may include:

- Duplexes, triplexes, and fourplexes. Here, you have multiple units in one structure and under one roof. As long as the homes are joined by a common wall and roofing structure and the structure does not have five or more units, the property likely qualifies as a "-plex" configuration. For new multi-family real estate investors, owning a "-plex" is one of the most accessible real estate forms. This is because it's possible to obtain a residential real estate loan to purchase these properties. In contrast, properties with five or more units require a commercial real estate loan.

- Bungalow courts. These are several small free-standing houses arranged around a central common garden. The bungalow court concept was the predominant form of multi-family housing in Southern California from the 1910s through the 1930s.

- Townhouses. The name usually applies to urban multi-floor structures that share their side walls with adjacent properties. They can also be called row houses because they often form a continuous row. Each structure has its own entrance and often a small front lawn and backyard as well. As the name suggests, townhouses are designed for high-density, urban environments with tall and narrow silhouettes. Many older townhouses were built as single-family dwellings, with the individual floors subsequently broken into individual apartments and rented out.

- Garden apartments. These are low-rise apartment buildings of one, two, or three stories in height, surrounded by lawns, trees, shrubbery, or gardens. Because of their space, many garden-style complexes have amenities like a clubhouse and pool.

- Multistory apartment buildings. These are free-standing structures with four or more stories and units.

- High-rise apartments. In the United States, anything above seven stories is considered a high rise. Of course, seven would be low in a big city like Manhattan, where the average building has 18 floors! In comparison, a skyscraper has 40 or more floors.

Apartment buildings can be huge. The Edifices Copan (Copan Building) in downtown São Paulo, Brazil, is 459 feet tall with 38 stories. One of the largest buildings in Brazil, it comprises 1,160 apartments and 70 street-level commercial establishments. Due to a large number of residents, the Brazilian postal service assigned the building its own postal code.

The tallest residential building in the world is Central Park Tower in Midtown Manhattan, New York City. At a height of 1,550 feet, the building contains 179 condominiums starting on the 32nd floor.

As of 2022, Dubai in the United Arab Emirates boasts five of the ten tallest residential buildings in the world. While high-rise residential buildings are located throughout the city, most are found in Dubai Marina, known as the "tallest block in the world" because of the number of high-rise residential buildings.

Imagine collecting those rent checks every month!

Generational Wealth

The highest and most powerful form of wealth is generational. This is wealth you create or inherit, which you pass down to your heirs. Most families' biggest source of generational wealth is the family home. The parents buy the house outright when they're newly married or spend the next 30 years paying off the mortgage. At the end of 30 years, they own the house free and clear, and the only payments they must make are the local real estate taxes and the utility bills.

While real estate values can fluctuate and don't always keep up with inflation, your family house will generally steadily appreciate in value year after year. So if you bought your home at 35 for $200,000, by the time you're ready to retire at age 65, it might be worth $500,000. And if you pass away at age 85, it might be worth $700,000 to your heirs, who could either sell it or live in it—and the mortgage has long since been paid!

Many families with investment income put their money into real estate, including vacant land. Vacant land does not earn income but will steadily appreciate in value over time.

You might wonder just how much land can one individual own?

Meet John Malone. As the owner of 2.2 million acres of land, he holds the title of the largest private landowner in the United States. His holdings in Florida, New Mexico, Maryland, Maine, New Hampshire, Colorado, and Wyoming represent an area twice the size of Rhode Island.

He made his money in media. He was CEO of Tele-Communications Inc., a cable, and media giant, for 24 years, from 1973 to 1996. He's the chairman and largest shareholder of Liberty Media. He also owns 28 percent of Discover Communications as well as 8 percent of the Atlanta Braves baseball team. Thanks to his media company assets and land ownership, in 2022, his net worth was a cool $9.2 billion.

After the Emmerson family at number two with 2.07 million acres, number three on the list is another media tycoon, Ted Turner, who owns 2 million acres. Most of the acreage is devoted to 17 sprawling Turner Ranches, which operate as working businesses, relying on bison herding, hunting and fishing, and ecotourism as principal enterprises.

At number four is a perfect example of generational wealth. In 1897, Mark Edward Reed married Irene Simpson, whose father owned a logging company in Washington state. When the elder Simpson died, Mark Reed took over the company. He quickly expanded it and kept buying more land for the company and himself. Reed died in 1933, and the family kept the business, first with Mark's son Sol Reed at the helm, then William G. Reed, then William G. Reed Jr., and then Douglas Reed.

The reclusive Reed family owns Simpson Investment Company and are the fourth-largest private landowners in the United States, owning 1.7 million acres of timberland in eight states across the Pacific Northwest and the South. The Reed family has owned the Green Diamond Resource Company for five generations.

In the Western world, the all-time champion of generational wealth is the House of Windsor—more commonly known as England's royal family. Think about it for a minute: Who pays for the castles, carriages, yachts, aircraft, pomp and circumstance, and the army of servants? Even if you're King Charles III himself, there's no way you can "earn" that kind of cash. It must be massive, passive income.

The generational wealth of the individuals in the royal family and the wealth of the title they may hold comes from many sources. Here are a few.

The Crown Estate. First established in 1760, the Crown Estate is a collection of lands and holdings in the United Kingdom belonging to the British monarch as a corporation sole, making it "the sovereign's public estate," which is neither government property nor part of the monarch's private estate.

As a real estate empire, the Crown Estate is one of the largest property managers in the UK, administering property worth £14.1 billion, with urban properties valued at £9.1 billion, representing most of the estate by value. The government pays 25 percent of the Crown Estate's profit back to the royal family under what is known as the "Sovereign Grant." In 2021, this was reported to be $99 million.

The Duchy of Cornwall. Founded in 1337, the Duchy of Cornwall is a portfolio of land, property, and assets held in trust for the Prince of Wales as heir to the throne. Prince Charles was the beneficiary until he became king, and now the

beneficiary is William, Prince of Wales.   In   2021,   the
duchy earned $24 million for William.

The Duchy of Lancaster. Since 1351, the Duchy of Lancaster
has been a portfolio of land, property, and assets held in trust
for the sovereign. Today, that's King Charles III. In 2021, the
duchy reported $27 million in profit.

Elizabeth II, the late queen of the United Kingdom, also owned
family real estate in a private capacity. Her holdings included
Balmoral Castle in Scotland, where she's interred, and
Sandringham House in Norfolk, England. The queen's other
major properties, including Windsor Castle, the Palace of
Holyroodhouse, and even Buckingham Palace, are owned by
the Crown Estate and did not belong to the queen herself.

Being a member of the House of Windsor is a good place to
be—but the only way you'll gain admittance is through
marriage! It is, however, a good example of generational
wealth built over time and carefully managed.

Chapter 7

Become an Investor

Whether you have chosen one career or multiple career paths, your goal is to create excess cash flow and assets not required for everyday expenses. Not only do you need a pool of funds for emergencies and things you want to do today, but also for retirement.

To accomplish this, your income must consistently exceed your expenses, thereby building up a nest egg of capital, and you need a plan for how to preserve your capital and make it grow.

Simply doing the bare minimum, which is to keep your cash locked in a safe or hidden under a mattress, is a bad game plan based on fear. Every year, because of inflation, the value of your cash dollar will decline in purchasing power. For example, if you put $1,000 under your mattress in 2000, by 2020, it would be worth only $614.38. Shocking right?

That's why you need to go above and beyond the bare minimum. You need to build a comfortable economic cushion. This is not a question solely about your income. You can be very successful, hold a well-paying job, and even own real estate, and still live from month to month with no cash cushion or savings. There's a name for such people: the *wealthy hand-to-mouth.* These households own sizable amounts of illiquid assets (assets that carry a transaction cost, such as housing or retirement accounts) but hold little or no liquid wealth. Others call them HENRYs (High Earners Not Yet Rich) or the "faux riche" (people who look rich but aren't).

The seminal research study on this group was done in 2014 by Greg Kaplan of Princeton University, Giovanni Violante of New York University, and Justin Weidner of Princeton University. In "The Wealthy Hand-to-Mouth," they found that 30 percent of households in the United States were living hand-to-mouth, and the vast majority of hand-to-mouth households—at least two-thirds of them—were *wealthy* hand-to-mouth, not poor hand-to-mouth.

Who are these people? Along with other insights, the authors highlighted three features.

1. Unlike younger, poor hand-to-mouth households, the wealthy hand-to-mouth tend to be in their early 40s with solid incomes.

2. The wealthy hand-to-mouth possess substantial amounts of real estate and retirement accounts. As previously stated, these illiquid assets carry a transaction cost to access, so when the economy dips, they tend to "tighten their belts" rather than sell assets.

3. Wealthy hand-to-mouth status is easier to escape than poor hand-to-mouth status.

Neither party keeps large balances of cash on hand, which can cause heavy amounts of stress in the event of a financial calamity.

Take note of the limitations of living a hand-to-mouth existence and structure your finances where your wealth allows you freedom regardless of the markets or economic conditions.

You eventually want to be in a position where you can afford to make a few highly speculative investments. This method of investing means buying a part of or owning an asset outright—real estate, a company, or a piece of art—and then holding that asset for a period while it appreciates or pays a dividend.

Consult your accountant or financial advisor before making any speculative moves with your money. You can only lose a certain percentage of your overall net worth before adversely affecting your finances.

Any time you invest, you're taking a risk. The basic rule is that every investment is a trade-off between risk and reward. The higher the risk, the higher the possible reward—but also the possibility of a total loss. The lower the risk, the lower the reward.

To get anywhere as an investor, you must learn to manage risk, not avoid it. Playing it safe and minimizing the risk by investing in nothing but government bonds will protect your capital but will not produce a very satisfying return. At the opposite end of the investing spectrum you have cryptocurrency. Investing in this form of digital money is very speculative and could result in a nice gain or a complete loss of your capital.

So, what is the process for evaluating how much risk you can safely take? Generally, investment advisors say that three factors determine this.

1. Your age. When you're young, you can accept more risk because if you lose your money, you have a lifetime ahead to recover. As you get older and approach retirement, you'll want to reduce your risk exposure because you have less time and less ability to make up for a loss.

2. Your responsibilities. If you're single and mobile, you can afford to take more chances with your money. If you've got a family to support and a mortgage to pay, you'll want to play it smart.

3. Your free cash. Any investment, no matter how safe or risky, should be made only with money you can afford to lose. Tapping into the equity of your home can cause you to lose the pillow beneath you head. In most instances, your primary residence should not be mortgaged to purchase stock. If you buy stock, you should do so with the understanding that your money may vanish. Of course, this is not often the case; the stock market is full of blue-chip companies that stay strong year after year. But it's also no stranger to seemingly robust companies that go bankrupt—a few examples in recent history include General Motors, Lehman Brothers, Worldcom, Enron,

Pacific Gas and Electric, and many more. Losses to shareholders have amounted to billions of dollars.

Value Investing

Some people have gotten extremely wealthy by doing nothing but making investments. The most well-known example is Warren Buffett, who has more than once occupied the position of the wealthiest individual in the world. The fact that "the Oracle of Omaha" has made investments year after year and has consistently come out on top, with much more reward than failure, is pretty amazing.

He could not have amassed his wealth by playing it safe and only investing in "blue chip" stocks like General Electric or IBM. The return simply would not have been sufficient. On the other hand, he rarely misjudges the risk. When he considers making a bet on a company—he only moves forward when he's convinced the risk is very low and the return will be high.

He has two rules of investing: "Rule number 1: Never lose money. Rule number 2: Don't forget rule number 1." Of course, Buffett has lost money plenty of times; he reportedly lost $23 billion during the financial crisis of 2008. Nor does this mean you should invest only in "safe" stocks that will provide a poor return.

Buffett is simply referring to a sensible investor's mindset when making financial decisions: Don't be frivolous by failing to do your homework. Never go into financial decisions thinking it's acceptable to lose money. If you gamble and lose your capital, you're out of the game. To stay in the game, you must maintain a winning average. This is called *capital preservation*.

So what separates an investor like Buffett from the day trader who "plays the stock market" and often loses as much as he wins?

The answers are *due diligence* and *patience*. I'll explain what that means.

Buffett is a value investor. The value investor is not looking for a quick profit. They don't play the market and try to determine which stocks will rise today and which will fall tomorrow. The value investor searches for assets—in this case, companies—undervalued by the marketplace. Their share price should be higher than it is now—not just in the short term, but for the foreseeable future. When you find such a company and invest in it more than anyone else, you can become a controlling owner.

But you might ask, "Is that all there is? Just spotting companies that are undervalued? That sounds easy. Anyone could do that, right?"

The challenge is that it takes *work*. Key information about a company and its true value is not always visible. You have to dig deep and spend time researching. There isn't a universally accepted way to determine intrinsic value, but it's most often estimated by analyzing a company's fundamentals. These include return on equity, company debt, profit margins, the degree to which the company produces a commodity, and company longevity. Buffett invests only in companies that have been active for at least ten years and can generate earnings for the next ten or twenty years.

The value investor chooses stocks solely based on their current intrinsic value, and holding these stocks is a long-term play where cash flow is king. The size of a company is irrelevant.

Through his holding company, Berkshire Hathaway, Buffett owns stock in many big, highly visible companies, including Apple, Inc., Bank of America, American Express, Chevron, Coca-Cola, Kraft Heinz, Occidental Petroleum, US Bancorp, and Hewlett Packard. He's also invested in obscure companies you've probably never heard of.

How long does Buffett hold a stock? His goal, he has said, is "forever." That is to say, he intends to hold as long as the company continues to provide value. Berkshire Hathaway does occasionally unload a company. As of May 2022, Berkshire Hathaway's stock portfolio was worth more than $300 billion. In the first quarter of the year, the company sold its stake in five companies—AbbVie, Bristol-Myers Squibb, Wells Fargo, Verizon, and Royalty Pharma.[18]

---

[18] USNews. https://money.usnews.com/investing/stock-market-news/articles/the-complete-berkshire-hathaway-portfolio

Of the many investing rules Warren Buffett has set for himself, one of the most important is that he invests only in businesses that he understands. This makes sense; after all, how can you evaluate a company and its key performance indicators when you don't know how the company makes a profit? Yet many people succumb to the "hot stock" scenario and invest in a company that their friend, or perhaps a self-styled expert on TV, says is going to "go through the roof." Meanwhile, the investor knows nothing about the company or industry and has no way of knowing when to buy or sell it.

Buffett makes concentrated bets on companies operating in areas where he's highly knowledgeable and confident, and that's a big part of what has made him such an incredibly successful investor over time. As John Divine noted in USNews, in terms of sectors, Berkshire Hathaway's major investment in Apple makes information technology his most heavily represented sector, constituting about 46 percent of the portfolio as of March 2022. Financial companies accounted for 27 percent of the portfolio, while consumer staples were the last to break double digits at 11 percent.

Buffett has said he doesn't invest in sectors in which he's not comfortable or has limited knowledge. He does not invest in healthcare and pharma stocks, specialized tech stocks, and commodities or basic materials, including companies that produce precious metals, base metals, building materials, and specialty chemicals. He does not buy gold, which he views as a decorative material without a core industrial purpose.

As he wrote in his 1996 annual Berkshire Hathaway shareholders' letter, "Intelligent investing is not complex, though that is far from saying that it's easy. What an investor needs is the ability to correctly evaluate selected businesses. Note that word 'selected': You don't have to be an expert on every company, or even many. You only have to be able to evaluate companies within your circle of competence. The size of that circle is not very important; knowing its boundaries, however, is vital."[19]

Buffett told Yahoo Finance, "Maybe 5 percent of the companies or 10 percent of the companies at most are within an area, my circle of competence. They're something I should be able to understand."[20]

And above all, remember that unlike the game of baseball, in which you must eventually swing at a pitch or be called out on strikes, in the game of investing, you can stand there and watch pitch after pitch sail by you. If you don't like what you see coming at you, just hold your bat—or rather, hold your money. Don't be rushed, and don't feel pressured. It's your money, and you need to be wise about where you spend it.

Venture Capital

The area of investing with the most risk and greatest reward is venture capital.

---

[19] https://www.berkshirehathaway.com/letters/1996.html
[20] Yahoo. https://www.yahoo.com/lifestyle/warren-buffett-baseball-stock-picking-212405020.html

VC funding is a highly speculative form of investing that includes throwing money at startups and other entrepreneurial businesses with the potential for substantial and rapid growth. For new companies with a limited operating history (under two years), venture capital is an increasingly essential source for raising money, especially if the founders lack access to capital markets, bank loans, or other debt instruments.

Venture capital is usually provided by wealthy investors, venture capital companies or funds, investment banks, and other financial institutions. Individuals who have amassed their wealth through various sources and who then provide funds are often called angel investors. They tend to be entrepreneurs themselves or executives recently retired from the business empires they've built.

When investing in a startup, VC funding is provided in exchange for equity in the company, and it isn't expected to be paid back on a planned schedule in the conventional sense, like a bank loan. VCs typically take a long-range view and invest, hoping to see outsized returns should the company be acquired or go public. When the company is sold, they get paid their equity share. If the company goes public, its investments are converted into stock, which they can either keep or sell. When investing in companies, VCs usually take only a minority stake—50 percent or less—thereby leaving the company's day-to-day control in the founders' hands.

Shark Tank is basically a forum for entrepreneurs to find angel investors—that is, one or more of the Sharks. At the end of the entrepreneur's pitch, you might hear one of the Sharks make an offer, such as "I'll give you $100,000 for 10 percent of your company." That means they think the company is worth $1 million. Sometimes, the founders have a problem if they reveal that other investors already own a portion of the company. If you've already sold 40 percent of your company to others, you're much less attractive as an investment opportunity.

Sometimes, on *Shark Tank,* you'll see that a Shark will offer a straight loan to be repaid with interest, just as if the Shark were a bank. This is an option for the entrepreneur. The benefit is that the owner does not surrender any equity in the company. The risk is that the loan must be repaid by a specified date, and if the entrepreneur defaults, they could lose their company.

You may also see an offer of a royalty on manufactured goods sold. Shark Kevin O'Leary does this quite often. The offer might be that the investor provides $100,000 in exchange for only 5 percent ownership of the company but wants a royalty of one dollar for every item sold until the $100,000 has been paid back. After that, the investor remains a 5 percent owner in perpetuity. The royalty structure means the entrepreneur is under less pressure to pay back the $100,000—he only needs to make payments when he actually sells the product and receives income, not on a fixed timetable.

Venture capital can be risky because a level of blind faith is involved. Founders seeking investors often have little more than an idea in their heads. Such was the case in 1994 when Jeff Bezos went looking for funds to launch Amazon.com. According to a 2018 article in *The Guardian*, of the 50 potential investors Bezos pitched, he failed to convince 38. Years later, a number of them still cannot bring themselves to talk about what life might have been like if they had taken a chance on Bezos and his crazy internet bookstore.

"I'm in touch with a few of them now," Bezos revealed in an onstage interview at a charity dinner in Washington, DC. "It's kind of a study in human nature. Some of them take it in their stride, and they recognize that they actually have ridiculously happy lives. Others of them just cannot talk about it—it's too painful."

The 22 original investors, who included Bezos's younger brother Mark and sister Christina, were each granted just under 1 percent of Amazon's stock on average. If they held on to all the shares, their stakes would have been worth up to $7 billion each in 2018, a return of 14 million percent.[21]

If you had bought $1,000 worth of stock at Amazon's first IPO in May 1997, by October 2022, your stake would be worth more than $1.1 million.[22]

---

[21] https://www.scmp.com/news/world/united-states-canada/article/2143375/1994-he-convinced-22-family-and-friends-each-pay

[22] https://www.fool.com/investing/2022/10/13/invested-1000-in-amazon-stock-at-ipo-how-much-now/#:~:text=The%20stock%20has%20since%20soared,more%20than%20%241.1%20million%20today.

That's the kind of story every investor wants to hear!

Then there's the flip side—the story of fraud in which billions of dollars go up in smoke.

Founded in 2003 by then-19-year-old Elizabeth Holmes, Theranos was a startup touted as a breakthrough health technology company. Holmes claimed that her compact automated device could perform rapid blood testing with just a drop of blood. If true, this would represent a huge leap forward in blood analysis technology. Thanks in part to the personal persuasive powers of Elizabeth Holmes, Theranos raised more than $700 million from venture capitalists and private investors, resulting in a valuation of $10 billion at its peak in 2014.

In 2015, medical research professor John Ioannidis, Eleftherios Diamandis, and investigative journalist John Carreyrou of The Wall Street Journal questioned the validity of Theranos's technology. Their allegations led to a flood of legal and commercial challenges from medical authorities, investors, the U.S. Securities and Exchange Commission, the Centers for Medicare and Medicaid Services, state attorneys general, former business partners, patients, and others. The company became a pariah, and by June 2016, Holmes's personal net worth—based wholly on the value of her company—had dropped from $4.5 billion to virtually nothing. After several years of struggle, lawsuits, and sanctions from CMS, what remained of the company was dissolved on September 4, 2018.

In January 2022, Holmes was found guilty of four counts of fraud, and in November of the same year, was sentenced to 11 years and 3 months in prison. Her partner and former company president, Sunny Balwani, was convicted on all 12 counts brought against him in July 2022. In December 2022, he was sentenced to 12 years and 11 months in prison and 3 years of probation.

In all, more than $600 million of investors' cash was lost in the company's downfall. Based on the documents publicly released as part of a lawsuit against Theranos, we know how large a loss many investors took.

Betsy Devos, then the U.S. secretary of education, lost a reported $100 million of her family's money. Media mogul Rupert Murdoch lost $125 million, while Wal-Mart heirs in the Walton family lost $150 million. Other notable figures who saw large amounts disappear included former defense secretary Jim Mattis, who lost $85 million, and former secretary of state Henry Kissinger, who invested $3 million, while his lawyer, Daniel Mosley, invested a further $6 million.

One reason why Holmes could dupe so many powerful, intelligent people was that they looked around and saw that other powerful, intelligent people had jumped on board, thus validating the company and its claims.

For example, according to reporter John Carreyrou, billionaire Rupert Murdoch viewed Theranos's other investors, including Cox Enterprises, the Atlanta-based conglomerate that invested $100 million, as a signal of legitimacy for the technology.

Murdoch, in turn, attracted other investors and was pivotal to the company's success.

Tech entrepreneur Larry Ellison, founder of Oracle, was introduced to Holmes by Don Lucas, the founder of Lucas Venture Group and one of the company's earliest backers. Analysts aren't sure how much he invested in the firm, although Elizabeth Holmes is said to have told other investors that Ellison was considering putting up $20 million.

Amazon or Theranos—which will it be? Due diligence is the process of appraising a company's current condition and its profit potential. It means getting a deep understanding of the target company, its liabilities, its assets, and its management. The company's founding team indicates its direction, making it doubly important to learn about these key players early in the deal process. You must do this yourself or hire a trusted person to do it for you. If there are obvious personality conflicts—or worse, conflicting values—you may want to think twice before separating yourself from your hard-earned cash.

Chapter 8

Become a Philanthropist

Charity vs. Philanthropy

While the words "charity" and "philanthropy" are often used interchangeably, there are significant differences. While they both involve giving money directly to people, causes, or non-profit organizations that help people, charitable gifts are an immediate response to a short-term need. An example would be donating to the Red Cross after a natural disaster or to the Muscular Dystrophy Association after a fund-raising telethon. Charitable gifts are usually made from a household's checking account, like any bill or daily expense.

While charity is focused on providing immediate relief to people and is often driven by emotions, philanthropy is focused on helping people and solving their problems over the long term. Philanthropy is more strategic and often involves making multiple gifts to people or organizations over several years.

The old adage "Give a man a fish and you feed him for a day; teach him to fish and you feed him for a lifetime" illustrates the difference between charity and philanthropy. Just for fun, for the purposes of this book, let's add a third option: "Set the man up in business with a fish farm, and he'll have an income stream that will help him engage in philanthropy."

To give to charity, you don't have to be wealthy. Many people from all walks of life contribute to charitable organizations. In fact, according to Qgiv.com, individuals who earn $25,000 or less donate the largest share (16.6 percent) of their income to charity. Of the various age groups, Millennials (anyone born between 1981 and 1996, which represents 25.9 percent of the US population) are the top donors by percentage of income: In 2020, 84 percent of Millennials gave to charity, donating an average of $481 across an average of 3.3 charitable organizations.[23]

Generally speaking, philanthropy is making significant donations from your capital designed to strengthen a population or organization over the long term. Philanthropy means donating large sums of money, and philanthropic donors usually have significant passive income and are engaged in investing.

Andrew Carnegie

In American history, the most significant figure in philanthropy was Andrew Carnegie.

---

[23] https://nonprofitssource.com/online-giving-statistics/

Born in Dunfermline, Scotland, in 1835, Andrew Carnegie was 12 years old when he emigrated to the United States with his parents in 1848. He was put to work as a bobbin boy in a Pittsburgh cotton factory, where he changed spools of thread in a cotton mill 12 hours a day, six days a week.

Thus, at a young age, he began his career with a subsistence-level paycheck job.

The next year, Carnegie became a telegraph messenger boy in the Pittsburgh Office of the Ohio Telegraph Company. A hard worker, within a year, he was promoted to operator. This was another subsistence-level paycheck job, but to Carnegie's immense good fortune, it came with an unexpected bonus.

Carnegie had little formal education, but he knew how to read—and he eagerly devoured any kind of book he could get his hands on. Meanwhile, during the 1850s and 1860s, a local retired military officer and businessman, Colonel James Anderson, had assembled a personal library of some 400 volumes. As an act of philanthropy, he opened his library to the local "working boys," who could come on Saturdays and check out a book for a week.

Young Carnegie was amazed by this philanthropic gesture and later wrote in his autobiography:

"My dear friend, Tom Miller, one of the inner circle, lived near Colonel Anderson and introduced me to him, and in this way the windows were opened in the walls of my dungeon through which the light of knowledge streamed in. Every day's toil and even the long hours of night service were lightened by the book which I carried about with me and read in the intervals that could be snatched from duty. And the future was made bright by the thought that when Saturday came a new volume could be obtained.... Books which would have been impossible for me to obtain elsewhere were, by his wise generosity, placed within my reach; and to him I owe a taste for literature which I would not exchange for all the millions that were ever amassed by man."[24]

Carnegie slowly worked his way up through the ranks of American industry and began making investments in newly forming companies, particularly in the steel industry. In 1892, at the age of 57, he founded the Carnegie Steel Company.

Fast-forward to the year 1901. Now 66 years of age and at the pinnacle of his success, he considered his legacy. Carnegie sincerely believed that the duty of a rich person was to live a modest lifestyle and that any "surplus" (as he put it) of money possessed by the person was best suited for re-circulation back into society where it could be used to support the greater good.

Carnegie decided to sell his company to banker John Pierpont Morgan, America's most important financial deal maker. They signed the papers on March 2, 1901, and Morgan formed the United States Steel Corporation. It was the first corporation in the world with a market capitalization of over $1 billion. The

---

[24] Andrew Carnegie. http://www.info-ren.org/projects/btul/exhibit/anderson.html

price for Carnegie Steel was $303,450,000, from which Andrew Carnegie received $203 million. This would be about $7 billion in 2020 dollars, which he added to his already considerable fortune.

Embracing the maxim "The man who dies thus rich dies disgraced," he set about to give away his cash. Until his death on August 11, 1919, he focused his energy on philanthropy. The list of projects and causes he supported would be enough to fill an entire book, so we'll highlight the libraries.

Remembering the profound impact that Colonel Anderson's library had made, Carnegie had long supported the creation of free public libraries. In 1883, the first of Carnegie's public libraries, Dunfermline Carnegie Library, opened in his birthplace, Dunfermline, Scotland. In the United States, the first Carnegie Library opened in 1889. It was located in Braddock, Pennsylvania, the site of one of the Carnegie Steel Company's mills.

Carnegie expressed his very clear opinions about charity versus philanthropy. In his 1889 article, "The Best Fields for Philanthropy," published in *The North American Review*, he wrote:

"It is ever remembered that one of the chief obstacles which the philanthropist meets in his efforts to do real and permanent good in this world is the practice of indiscriminate giving, and the duty of the millionaire is to resolve to cease giving to objects that are not proved clearly to his satisfaction to be deserving. He must remember Mr. Rice's belief, that nine hundred and 50 out of every thousand dollars bestowed today upon so-called charity had better be thrown into the sea."[25]

Carnegie believed that habitual "beggars" were weakened and made even more destitute by receiving free assistance. He did not address the issue of emergency aid to those who have suffered an abrupt and life-threatening loss.

Libraries are resources that the user must seek out. They don't come to you. In fact, all Carnegie libraries were designed with two features: You entered by ascending a set of stairs, signifying your intellectual elevation, and by the front door hung a lantern, signifying enlightenment. He also required that the host city or town provide funds for the operation and upkeep of the library that Carnegie would build for them. This was a requirement because Carnegie wanted the town to have "skin in the game"—that is, to share the commitment to the project's success. Carnegie's maxim could have been to "help those who help themselves."

Between 1883 and 1929, a total of 2,509 Carnegie libraries were constructed, including some belonging to public and university library systems. Most were built in the United States, many in the United Kingdom, Ireland, and Canada, and

---

[25] Andrew Carnegie.
https://digitallibrary.punjab.gov.pk/jspui/bitstream/123456789/125328/1/The%20g ospel%20of%20wealth%20essays%20and%20other%20writings%20%28%20PDFD rive%20%29.pdf

others in Australia, South Africa, New Zealand, Serbia, Belgium, France, the Caribbean, Mauritius, Malaysia, and Fiji.

Other Carnegie philanthropic institutions include the Carnegie Institute of Technology (CIT) in Pittsburgh (now known as Carnegie Mellon University) and the Carnegie Institution in Washington, D.C. Andrew Carnegie built and owned Carnegie Hall in New York City and contributed $1.5 million for the construction of the Peace Palace at The Hague.

Carnegie died on August 11, 1919, in Lenox, Massachusetts. He had given away over $350 million during his lifetime—an amount that, converted to 2020 terms, would equal nearly $80 billion. After his death, and after providing for his widow Louise Whitfield Carnegie and their daughter Margaret Carnegie Miller, his last $30 million was distributed to foundations, charities, and pensioners.

His impact has been lasting. In the United States, 1,689 public libraries were built thanks to Carnegie grants. Over a century later, about 750 are still functioning as libraries.

These days, philanthropy continues in many forms. Among the very wealthy, the "Giving Pledge" has become popular. This well-publicized campaign encourages the top one percent to contribute at least half their wealth to philanthropic causes. As of June 2022, the pledge had 236 signatories from 28 countries. According to the *Chronicle of Philanthropy*, giving by the 50 biggest donors in the United States totaled $24.7

billion in 2020, with Jeff Bezos's $10.15 billion in giving topping the list.[26]

How You Can Help: Time, Talent, and Treasure

If you have a vision for providing sustained assistance to a charitable organization, you can get started even if you aren't a billionaire and don't yet have a pile of cash to give away.

We'll get to that soon. But first, let's start with the basics.

In the United States, a charity is an organization recognized by the Internal Revenue Service as providing a service to the community that the government would otherwise provide, and therefore your donation to that organization is tax deductible. Most charities carry an IRS 501(c)(3) designation, and are operated exclusively for religious, charitable, scientific, testing for public safety, literary, educational, or other specified purposes. If you're not sure if the organization that interests you is a legitimate charity, several watchdog websites can help you, such as GuideStar.org and CharityNavigator.org.

In the early stages of your exploration into philanthropy, one of the first questions you're likely to have is, "What charitable

---

[26] Philanthropy News. https://philanthropynewsdigest.org/news/billionaire-philanthropy-is-a-pr-scam-wealth-tax-proponent-argues

organizations should I support? Where can I make a difference?"

It's likely there will be a wide variety of causes that you care about. That's fine—many donors start by learning about the various charitable organizations operating in their town or nationally. These may include non-profits in these industries:

- Religion: churches, synagogues, mosques.

- Healthcare: hospitals, clinics, family planning.

- Social service: homeless shelters, soup kitchens, thrift shops, libraries.

- Education: non-profit schools and universities.

- Culture: museums, theaters, art centers, ballet, opera, classical music.

- Veterans' groups that serve former military.

- Animal shelters and charities.

A good way to get started is to ask yourself a few questions: What people, problems, places, or pathways do I care most about? What do I like or dislike about the organization, and perhaps more importantly, what organization aligns with my purpose, values, and philosophies?

And then there's the question of how you contribute—and it's not just by writing a check. There are three ways people just like you can become philanthropic. They are known as the "three Ts": time, talent, and treasure. Let's see how you can make them a part of your life.

Time

Most charitable organizations have a mechanism that makes it easy to volunteer because they regularly need new recruits. Every charitable organization needs volunteers. From your local soup kitchen or Goodwill store to the well-endowed fine arts museum, you can find a role as a volunteer that does not require special training.

As for tax implications, the IRS doesn't allow you to deduct the time you spend doing volunteer work. You choose to give your time to support the organization freely, and you can't assign a value to that time or the services you provide and deduct it from your tax return.

But when you use a personal vehicle to get to and from the place you volunteer, you can deduct mileage and travel expenses, including the miles you drive providing transportation, delivering meals, or any driving you do that is directly related to the volunteer work.

Talent

If you have a professional skill or qualification, you can use it in the service of a non-profit. Usually, this is done at the board level. Non-profit boards oversee the charity's operation, which could be anything from a local rape crisis center to a multi-million-dollar hospital or museum. Boards need to get things done, including financial reports, legal issues, special events planning, real estate development, human resources questions, etc. For example, you'll find a lawyer and an accountant on nearly every non-profit board. On hospital boards, you'll find doctors, and on school boards, you'll find educators.

As with any other volunteering, your time is not tax-deductible, but out-of-pocket expenses can be. Other types of business donations, such as products, inventory, and cash donations, can be deducted. Businesses should use the fair market value of those donations when including them on their tax returns.

Treasure

Treasure includes cash donations as well as donations of real estate, stocks and other securities, motor vehicles, and artwork. There are many ways to donate: Write a check, establish a trust, leave the organization a bequest in your will, or solicit donations from well-heeled friends and family members.

At the higher levels of philanthropic giving, you'll want to take advantage of the advice of a tax attorney or financial planner.

Wealthy or well-established non-profit boards tend to be strict about the time, talent, or treasure rule: If you don't have a specifically needed talent or can't devote much time to the board's work, you're expected to pony up the cash. If you can't write a check yourself, you're expected to solicit donations from friends, family, or your business.

The most prestigious non-profit boards require substantial cash donations from board members. In New York, the nation's cultural capital, the Metropolitan Museum of Art reportedly requires an initial donation of at least $10 million. The Metropolitan Opera looks for at least $250,000, Alvin Ailey Dancers expects at least $10,000, and the Museum of Natural History wants $75,000—all in addition to regular annual donations. Of course, the benefits of becoming a trustee include opportunities to socialize with the wealthy and famous and enhanced social status and influence. These board seats also bring obligations such as approving programs and annual budgets, investing the endowment, and managing the physical properties.

In Closing

The time has come to decide what the preceding information on *Career Reinvention* will mean to your future. Committing to reinventing your career can be scary at times, especially when things start happening to stretch your paradigm. Be brave concerning the inevitable changes that will take place as your work life begins to take on a different shape.

If you are thrilled with where you are currently employed and merely seek to improve your life by producing more income, take action to create one new income stream per year involving self-employment or passive income. This one goal can eventually change your entire future! If you take action on it regularly.

As for the remaining group of people eyeballing other opportunities, kick-start your *Career Reinvention* process by reassessing your current situation daily, weekly, monthly, or yearly. Ask yourself these relevant questions: on a scale of one to ten, how satisfied am I with my current career? Does my work situation provide for my happiness and well-being now and in the future? Chances are, if you need to ask these questions, you are somewhat dissatisfied with your work life. Dwell on the feelings your subconscious gives you and use that as fuel to change your existing paradigm.

As challenges arise, re-familiarize yourself with the benefits of the DAPVEA method in Chapter 2. This strategy will change who you are—if it is used regularly.

We are creatures of habit and conduct our lives according to our beliefs. Do you believe you are capable of much greater works in life? If not, use the DAPVEA method to imprint the belief into your subconscious.

When seeking to reinvent your career, have you definitively identified your desire and stated an auto-suggestion, such as "I am reinventing my career?" Have you formed a positive affirmation concerning your desire? Have you visualized what an end result of your desire would look like? Is there an emotional component to your desire, or do you need to create one? Have you identified actions that might bring you closer to your desire?

Have you written down your desire to reinvent your career? Are you motivated enough to begin taking action on your desire to create a higher line, or lines, of income? If not, find things that inspire you and keep them in the forefront of your mind, where they can become embedded into your subconscious, where autonomous actions will be taken toward your desire. If you are a person who resists change, impregnating your subconscious mind with your desire may be the only way to create positive change in your behavior patterns.

More detailed information on using the DAPVEA method can be found in my book titled, *Six-Steps to Goal Achievement: Achieve Your Goals with These Six Easy Steps*. A later chapter in the book is titled "A Goal Encoding Frenzy," if that chapter doesn't light your fire, your wood is wet. *Six-Steps to Goal Achievement* can be found on Amazon and other publishing platforms in three formats: e-books, print books, and audiobooks.

Six-Steps to Goal Achievement is a must-read for anyone struggling with an unrealized goal. Reference the knowledge in both of these books and keep identifying actions you can take to improve your career. The more effort put into conditioning your mind to the premise you can reinvent your career, the higher lines of income you will understand how to access.

Focused searching, more education, and more networking will continue to reveal ever-increasing opportunities for finding your dream job, side gig, or even self-employment. As you seize new opportunities, you will feel relieved that you are on the way to climbing the ladder of success. The fact is that opportunities abound in the United States and other countries, as well. No matter where you are starting from, you have access to the same infrastructure that assisted many people in becoming financially comfortable.

Having established higher lines of income and understanding the financial benefits of investing, you can put a percentage, or increased percentage, of your money to work by regularly investing in assets that produce passive income. By building up your passive income, you can now take more vacations, spend more time with your family, and relax.

With your increased wealth and time freedom, you'll spot charitable or philanthropic opportunities that will make a difference in others' lives. Making a difference in other peoples' lives will result in great personal satisfaction.

Whatever direction you take your career in, remember this: you only live once, so do whatever you do with a sense of urgency. New opportunities are right before you; all you need to do is take deliberate actions toward them, and they will reveal themselves to you.

Your quest for *Career Reinvention* begins now.

About The Author

Dennis J. Dwyre is a business owner and creator of the Self-Help Strategist LLC publishing brand. After years of sheer hard work and becoming convinced that "there has to be a better way," he discovered the innate six steps to goal achievement method. His thirst for knowledge drove him to attend numerous workshops, programs, and seminars on personal development, finances, real estate, business, health, writing, publishing, and branding. His mission is to share the wisdom he's gained with as many people as possible while sowing seeds of inspiration and transformation.

Show Someone Else the Way Forward

*"Wisdom from sages, over the ages, are delivered through pages."—**Dennis J. Dwyre***

I am sincerely grateful for your time and commitment to meeting with me here within these pages. Now that you've digested this information on *Career Reinvention*, have you found it beneficial?

If so, one small act of charity can influence others to secure their own copy.

An Amazon review contribution will let readers know how this book has helped you and the type of guidance they'll find inside. You'll be helping other individuals to recognize they, too, can reinvent their careers.

Simply scan one of these QR code below and you will be seamlessly directed to this book's reviews page.

US	UK	Ca	Au

I sincerely thank you in advance.

End Notes

1 Forbes. https://www.forbes.com/sites/laurashin/2014/02/03/cant-leave-a-miserable-job-because-of-the-money-take-these-7-steps/?sh=46e94cb73069

2 https://www.creditkarma.com/about/commentary/inflation-brings-to-the-fore-pay-inequities-this-equal-pay-day

3 https://ir.lendingclub.com/news/news-details/2022/48-Percent-of-Americans-with-Annual-Incomes-over-100000-Live-Paycheck-to-Paycheck-9-percentage-points-higher-than-first-reported-in-June-2021/default.aspx

4 OSU. https://news.osu.edu/lousy-jobs-hurt-your-health-by-the-time-youre-in-your-40s/

5 Oshio T. Job dissatisfaction as a predictor of poor health among middle-aged workers: a 14-wave mixed model analysis in Japan. Scand J Work Environ Health. 2021 Nov 1;47(8):591-599. doi: 10.5271/sjweh.3985.

Epub 2021 Sep 14. PMID: 34518892; PMCID: PMC9058618.

6 https://www.canada.ca/en/financial-consumer-agency/services/financial-wellness-work/stress-impacts.html

7 NYT. https://www.nytimes.com/2022/05/19/business/wells-fargo-fake-interviews.html

8 CBS News. https://www.cbsnews.com/news/linkedin-ceo-jeff-weiner-on-microsoft-acquisition-management-style-and-the-perfect-profile/

9 CNBC.com. https://www.cnbc.com/2019/10/05/apple-ceo-steve-jobs-technology-is-nothing-heres-what-it-takes-to-achieve-great-success.html

10 https://www.mercurynews.com/2015/04/01/the-story-of-gary-dahl-and-the-pet-rock-from-the-archives/

11 Griswald, Wesley S. (January 1966). "Can You Invent a Million-Dollar Fad?" Popular Science. 188 (1): 78–81.

12 CNBC.com. https://www.cnbc.com/2018/08/02/how-jeff-bezos-got-his-parents-to-invest-in-amazon--turning-them-into.html

13 https://timeline.com/gm-invented-planned-obsolescence-cc19f207e842

14 Hoffmann, Frank W.; William G. Bailey (1994). Fashion & Merchandising Fads. Routledge.pp. 243–244. ISBN 1-56024-376-7.

15 ESPN. https://www.espn.com/college-football/story/_/id/13789009/royalties-gatorade-inventors-surpass-1-billion

16 https://www.celebritynetworth.com/richest-businessmen/producers/dick-wolf-net-worth/

17 https://www.theceomagazine.com/business/finance/richest-family-walton-walmart/

18 Toptal.com. https://www.toptal.com/finance/real-estate/wall-street-buying-single-family-homes

19 USNews. https://money.usnews.com/investing/stock-market-news/articles/the-complete-berkshire-hathaway-portfolio

20 https://www.berkshirehathaway.com/letters/1996.html

21 Yahoo. https://www.yahoo.com/lifestyle/warren-buffett-baseball-stock-picking-212405020.html

22 https://www.scmp.com/news/world/united-states-canada/article/2143375/1994-he-convinced-22-family-and-friends-each-pay

23 https://www.fool.com/investing/2022/10/13/invested-1000-in-amazon-stock-at-ipo-how-much-now/#:~:text=The%20stock%20has%20since%20soared,more%20than%20%241.1%20million%20today.

24 Maslow. https://psychclassics.yorku.ca/Maslow/motivation.htm

25 https://nonprofitssource.com/online-giving-statistics/

26 Andrew Carnegie. http://www.info-ren.org/projects/btul/exhibit/anderson.html

27 Andrew Carnegie.
https://digitallibrary.punjab.gov.pk/jspui/bitstream/123456789/125328/1/T
he%20gospel%20of%20wealth%
20essays%20and%20other%20writings%20%28%20PDFDrive%2
0%29.pdf

28 Philanthropy News.
https://philanthropynewsdigest.org/news/billionaire-philanthropy-is-a-pr-
scam-wealth-tax-proponent-argues

Made in the USA
Columbia, SC
19 January 2025